One of the fastest developing areas of science lies in discoveries about the human brain, about which we knew almost nothing only a few decades ago. Now the implications of that knowledge are spreading into other disciplines. *The Rise of the Australian Neurohumanities: Conversations Between Neurocognitive Research and Australian Literature* is the first edited volume to explore the implications of this study for the reading and writing of Australian literature. Bridging neuroscience and the humanities, this diverse collection of essays adds to our understanding of issues such as empathy, voice, narrative persuasion, and the relation between our brains and body when enjoying esthetic experiences. It provides a new direction in Australian literary and cultural studies.

Dennis Haskell, *AM, The University of Western Australia*

Bringing together cognitive literary studies and Australian literary studies in a sustained and detailed way, this collection skillfully draws on a wide range of recent empirical and theoretical work on cognition, neuroscience, emotion, and sociality to address central issues and themes in Australian literary studies, among them the bearing of settler and indigenous discourse, experience, and histories on one another, the challenges of reconfiguring national identity in multi-ethnic, multi-cultural directions, the place of the wilderness and interactions with the environment in imaginative, affective life and ideological constructs, and the positioning of contemporary fiction in relation to a colonizing past and a globalized, post-national future.

Donald R. Wehrs, *Hargis Professor of English Literature, Auburn University, USA*

T0347475

The Rise of the Australian Neurohumanities

This exciting one-of-a-kind volume brings together new contributions by geographically diverse authors who range from early career researchers to well-established scholars in the field.

It unprecedentedly showcases a wide variety of the latest research at the intersection of Australian literary studies and cognitive literary studies in a single volume.

It takes Australian fiction on the leading edge by paving the way for a new direction in Australian literary criticism.

Jean-François Vernay is the author of *Water from the Moon: Illusion and Reality in the Works of Australian Novelist Christopher Koch* (Cambria Press, 2007), *A Brief Take on the Australian Novel* (Wakefield Press, 2016), *The Seduction of Fiction* (Palgrave Macmillan, 2016), and *La séduction de la fiction* (Hermann, 2019).

Routledge Focus on Literature

For more information about this series, please visit: https://www.
routledge.com/Routledge-Focus-on-Literature/book-series/RFLT

The Rise of the Australian Neurohumanities

Conversations Between Neurocognitive Research and Australian Literature

Edited by
Jean-François Vernay

Routledge
Taylor & Francis Group

NEW YORK AND LONDON

First published 2021
by Routledge
605 Third Avenue, New York, NY 10158

and by Routledge
2 Park Square, Milton Park, Abingdon, Oxon, OX14 4RN

Routledge is an imprint of the Taylor & Francis Group, an informa business

Library of Congress Cataloging-in-Publication Data
Names: Vernay, Jean-François, editor.
Title: The rise of the Australian neurohumanities : conversations between neurocognitive research and Australian literature / edited by Jean-François Vernay.
Description: New York, NY : Routledge, 2021. | Series: Routledge focus on literature | Includes bibliographical references and index. |
Identifiers: LCCN 2020052874 | ISBN 9780367751944 (hardback) | ISBN 9781003161424 (ebook)
Subjects: LCSH: Australian fiction--20th century-- Psychological aspects. | Australian fiction--21st century-- Psychological aspects. | Philosophy of mind in literature. | Creativity in literature.
Classification: LCC PR9612.6.P79 R57 2021 | DDC 823.009/ 994–dc23
LC record available at https://lccn.loc.gov/2020052874

ISBN: 978-0-367-75194-4 (hbk)
ISBN: 978-0-367-77535-3 (pbk)
ISBN: 978-1-003-16142-4 (ebk)

Typeset in Times New Roman
by MPS Limited, Dehradun

Contents

Contributors

Francesca Di Blasio lectures at the University of Trento, Italy. Her areas of research are literary theory, Indigenous Australian literature, early modern literature, and modernism. Di Blasio has been working for over a decade, continues to work on Indigenous Australian literature and the post(?)-colonial gaze, and is the author of various works on this topic. She has translated Oodgeroo Noonuccal's *We Are Going* (Trento 2013) and Rita and Jackie Huggins' *Auntie Rita* (Verona 2018) into Italian. Di Blasio is the president of the Italian Association for Australian and South Pacific Studies (AISAO – *Associazione Italiana di Studi sull'Australia e sull'Oceania*).

Dorothee Klein is a lecturer and research assistant in the department of English literatures and cultures at the University of Stuttgart. Her research interests include Australian studies, Aboriginal literatures, postcolonial theory, and (cognitive) narratology. She has published articles on Aboriginal life-writing, contemporary Aboriginal fiction and short-story cycles, and unnatural narratology. Her book *Poetics and Politics of Relationality in Contemporary Australian Aboriginal Fiction* will be published by Routledge in 2021.

Lukas Klik is currently a lecturer and Ph.D. candidate at the University of Vienna. His main research interests are contemporary Australian fiction and narrative theory. In his Ph.D. project, he focuses on contemporary Australian multiperspectival novels and analyses and how they reflect the diversification of present-day Australia through their form. He has published an article on Kim Scott in *ARIEL: A Review of International English Literature* and book reviews in *Journal of Australian Studies* and *Australian Literary Studies*. Recently, he has co-guest-edited a special issue on "Disturbances of the Home/land in Anglophone Postcolonial Literatures," published in *Humanities*.

Victoria Reeve undertook doctoral studies on the poetics of the novel form out of a deep interest in the imaginative and intellectual achievements of literary work of art and a strong desire to write literary fiction herself. She has written various articles on Australian fiction and the role of emotion in the literary text. She is undertaking a Master of Arts in Creative Writing at The University of Tasmania. The creative component of her thesis is a novella that makes use of multiple instances of perspective-taking in the form of sign-posted head-hopping, as a means to providing greater scope for reader empathy and engagement with character.

Rocío Riestra-Camacho is a Ph.D. candidate at the University of Oviedo, where she researches the cognitive bibliotherapeutic potential of young adult sports fiction in the treatment of anorexia. She has recently set up a reading experiment at the University of Oxford to investigate this. Riestra-Camacho holds a degree in English studies from the University of Oviedo, having been awarded the Extraordinary End of Studies Degree Prize. She finished her MA in gender studies at the University of Utrecht. She also holds an MA in ESL Pedagogy from the Spanish Distance Education University, and is now enrolled in psychology at the same institution.

Lisa Smithies completed a Ph.D. in 2018 at the University of Melbourne, where she continues to teach creative writing. Her research aims to illuminate creative writing practice through the application of scientific theories, particularly regarding cognition and linguistics. Lisa has won awards for both her academic and creative publications and is currently working on a monograph, titled *Writing DNA*. In her own creative practice, she writes flash fiction, short fiction, and screenplays.

Jean-François Vernay is the author of *Water from the Moon: Illusion and Reality in the Works of Australian Novelist Christopher Koch* (Cambria Press, 2007), *A Brief Take on the Australian Novel* (Wakefield Press, 2016), *The Seduction of Fiction: A Plea for Putting Emotions Back into Literary Interpretation* (Palgrave Macmillan, 2016), and *La séduction de la fiction* (Hermann, 2019). His new monograph, *Neurocognitive Interpretations of Australian Literature: Criticism in the Age of Neuroawareness*, is forthcoming in the Routledge Focus series. Most of his books are either available in translation or in the process of being translated.

Sue Woolfe lectures on creativity at the National Institute of Dramatic Art, and also at the School of Music in The Australian National University. She is a prize-winning novelist and short story writer;

her books include the best-selling and internationally awarded *Leaning Towards Infinity* (Random 1996). Her most recent fiction is *Do You Love Me or What?* (Simon and Schuster, 2017). Her non-fiction includes *Making Stories: How Ten Australian Novels Were Written* (with Kate Grenville, A&U, 1991) and *The Mystery of the Cleaning Lady: A Writer Looks at Creativity and Neuroscience,* (UWA, 2007). She has published several articles on writing and neuroscience.

Foreword

Reverberating throughout this captivating collection of essays, the voices of *The Rise of the Australian Neurohumanities* compel the reader to engage in conversation with urgent questions relating to the environment, equality, public health, and postcolonialism. Most significantly, the authors address these issues through a discussion of how we write, read, understand, and possibly seek to resolve them through literature. The work's title presents the academic essays as "conversations" that aptly reflect the dynamic, embodied experience of hearing the strong voices of the scholars and reflectively listening and responding to the challenges they throw down. While this is ostensibly a book about Australian literature, it is a powerful statement about the human experience and its expression in a modern world, which is more ubiquitously relevant.

In his comprehensive overview of cognitive literary studies in the Australian context, Jean-François Vernay modestly refers to the first wave of the "cognitive turn" criticism reaching Australia a decade after its initial impact in the United States, and suggests that the Australian neurohumanities are "just getting into their stride." However, it is probably more accurate, metaphorically speaking, to say that in this instance the Australian neurohumanities are breaking into a gallop. The essays of this collection clearly advance previous scholarship in significant ways which will influence future work in the field. While the authors contextualize the research questions of each chapter in current theory, each essay demonstrates by precise textual analysis how the theory relates to the reading and writing process with specific examples, and invariably draws new conclusions, or identifies new problems, which set the stage for new questions and further research. Several of the essays make significant contributions to affect studies, with Reeve and Di Blasio in their analyses of emotion as cognition outlining the interface between the individual's mind and the world external to it. As Reeve writes, "Emotions as categories have a specific focus, organizing such relations in terms of culturally recognizable feeling states and their associated actions, affects and effects." Smithies explores a similar line of inquiry in an essay which considers narrative voice in the context of embodied cognition, emphasizing voice which "bridges our internal and external worlds" as belonging to both the body and the mind. She coins the term "storyvoice" to describe the culmination of paralanguage, inner language and hypostasis in a voice for the storyworld, which is integral to its construction. By including an essay by the Australian novelist, Sue Woolfe, Vernay gives us a new perspective on neurocreativity as he highlights the unique contribution creative writers make to the neurohumanities because of their understanding of the writing process. It is also worth noting resonances between the essays of the collection, which strike highly suggestive chords. For example, Smithies discusses Theory of Mind in relation to the child Billy in *The Cold Snap*, noting that, in the absence of Billy's understanding, the reader supplies this information by shifting positions, which recalls Klik's essay on the reader's role in the multiperspectival novels *The Slap* and *Five Bells*. The final essay of the collection by Klein examines the ways in which Aboriginal literature provokes bodily reactions in the reader through careful, rhythmic use of language, thus reinforcing albeit in a very different context Riestra-Camacho's description of verbal motor resonance in her essay on children's sports literature.

One of the most rewarding aspects of *The Rise of Australian Neurohumanities* is the collection's ease in moving from theory and literature to the real-world impacts of human textual expression. For example, Di Blasio foregrounds the transformative power of esthetic emotion in her discussion of *Taboo* in which the characters come to terms with the violence of the past through storytelling. Woolfe's essay on the neuroscientific basis of creativity from a novelist's perspective offers insights into the creative process for artists who encounter obstacles and blocks. Analyzing linguistic motor resonance in a popular children's book, Riestra-Camacho's essay proposes a "narrative-persuasion-in-health" approach to childhood obesity. Klik's analysis of *The Slap* proposes that the multiperspectival focalizing of the novel foregrounds empathy with marginalized subjectivities.

While Vernay emphasizes the utility of cognitive literary approaches to re-invigorating Australian literary studies, it is also arguably just as significant that this collection of essays introduces readers to the rich contemporary Australian literature it explores so thoroughly. From the essays emerges a distinct, enthralling presentation of modern, uniquely Australian fiction, featuring indelible characters such as Billy, the neuro-atypical child of *The Cold Snap*, who protects the gum trees;

the high leaping child football player, Specky Magee; Jude, a disenfranchised, middle-aged woman, who recoils in disgust from "lambs' brains on a plate"; Tilly and her twin relatives Gerald and Gerard, who reconnect with "the rhizomatic roots of Noongar storytelling" when they travel to Kepalup for the opening of the Peace Park in recognition of a historical massacre of the Noongar, traversing land where "the kangaroo [is] peeping in and out of sight."

Paula Leverage,
School of Languages and Cultures,
Center for Neuro Humanities,
Purdue University

Preface

Jean-François Vernay

The brain-based economy, in which the fast-moving field of neuro-science is playing an important part, is gradually making its mark on academia and is likely to supersede the idea of a knowledge-based economy. This is perhaps one of the main reasons why cognitive literary studies are having a growing influence on the humanities, mainly in the United States, in Europe, and in China. By introducing cognitive methodologies and explanatory frameworks into the field of literary criticism and by adopting a perspective which reconfigures the entire field of literary studies, cognitive literary studies are optimistically on their way to finding their pertinence in our increasingly neuro-aware society.

The close association between literature and the brain is a most natural, if not symbiotic, one. Respectively in a figurative and in a literal way, literature and the brain are the seat of thought and emotions. Literature invites readers to peep in the innermost recesses of the human psyche and indulge in the meretricious pleasures of sentimentality. As is the case with literature, "learning about the brain is a venture that has no finishing line or point of completion. There's always going to be more to know" (Dingman 211). The main reason for it is that both literature and the brain are in a state of constant flux and change. Furthermore, literature – very much like the brain again – is subordinated to language and imitation, two processes without which it cannot evolve. What is more, whether it is thought of as a practice or as a reader's experience, literature is a highly cognitive discipline which is putting to good use the brain's five basic cognitive functions: perception, attention, language, emotion, and memory. Being the result of the brain's creative and fabulating abilities as well as a source for further creative and fabulating activities which lie at the basis of counterfactual scenarios, one could even argue that literature as an ever-expanding archive epitomizes the extension of our brain's cognitive capacity.

This push to reconcile science with the humanities and redefine literature as a rich cognitive artifact is all the more important today in Australia where the humanities are being de-emphasized so as to give precedence to STEM education. At a time when interdisciplinarity has become an imperative in Australian Universities, cognitive Australian literary studies are increasingly gaining visibility in the publishing arena worldwide with its growing number of theoretical works that blend scientific approaches with literary critical practice. Besides offering an extraordinary opportunity to bridge the "gulf of mutual incomprehension" (Snow 4) between literary intellectuals and scientists – one that novelist-cum-scientist Charles Percy Snow famously identified in the wake of World War II – this polymorphous field could even share "the excitement of connecting scientific principles with a love of literature" (Stockwell 11).

While the cognitive turn was heralded by a spate of seminal publications which started being released in the United States in the early 1990s, it was not before another decade that this first wave of scholarship would have repercussions in Australia. The time has therefore come to talk about the rise of the Australian neurohumanities and to keep the conversation going between neurocognitive research and Australian literature. Along with expanding the zone of contact between literary studies and brain science, this Routledge volume aims at blurring the boundaries between Australian literary studies and cognitive literary studies. This edited collection of essays, like all new contributions to this field, attests to the ever-increasing popularity of cognitivism and to its influence on various disciplines, including those in the humanities. All eight international contributors to this volume have built on the massive scaffolding that cognitive studies have developed over 50 years of research while also opening new avenues of inquiry and creating "new heuristic constellations," as Elleke Bohemer has it (Bohemer 584). I have deliberately chosen to include in this volume a cross section of most strains which compose cognitive literary studies: cognitive literary history (Jean-François Vernay), affective literary theory (Lukas Klik, Victoria Reeve, and Francesca Di Blasio), and Neuro Lit Crit (Lisa Smithies, Sue Woolfe, and Rocío Riestra-Camacho). Finally, this collection of essays is capped off with forays into cognitively informed preexisting theories (Dorothee Klein).

All scholars have contributed passionately to this ongoing conversation, whether by thoroughly exploring the scholarly work of their favorite neuroscientist through years of commitment or by opening up a productive exchange between the humanities and neurocognitive research. Indeed, in an exercise of metacognition, Sue Woolfe is having a conversation with her creative self by dialoguing with the theoretical findings of Liane Gabora, for whom she has confessed to have a profound admiration. Some contributors, such as Rocío Riestra-Camacho and Lisa Smithies, have taken our call for chapters as an opportunity to extend their passion for cognitive literary studies to the field of Australian literary studies. Others, like Francesca Di Blasio and Lukas Klik, have gone through the reverse journey by taking their Ozlit expertise into neurocognitive territory. As to Dorothee Klein, Victoria Reeve, Sue Woolfe, and myself, we are prolonging our interest in cognitive Australian literary studies and just adding to the initial conversation by building on our previous scholarly work in the field.

This exciting collection of thought-provoking essays ambitiously aims at showing that the Australian neurohumanities are just getting into their stride and hold the promise of offering much more in the years to come. It is to be hoped that *The Rise of the Australian Neurohumanities: Conversations Between Neurocognitive Research and Australian Literature* is just a conversation starter that will keep the stimulating debate going.

Works Cited

Boehmer, Elleke. "Response to Michela Borzaga: Postcolonial Poetics." *Journal of Postcolonial Writing*, vol. 56, no. 4, 2020, pp. 583–584.

Dingman, Marc. *Your Brain, Explained: What Neuroscience Reveals About Your Brain and Its Quirks*. Nicholas Brealey Publishing, 2019.

Snow, Charles Percy. *The Two Cultures*. Cambridge UP, 1998.

Stockwell, Peter. *Cognitive Poetics: An Introduction*. Routledge, 2002.

Acknowledgments

My warmest gratitude goes to Paula Leverage, our foreword author, and to the following reviewers, who have all been most generous with their time, expertise, and uplifting support.

Cognitive Literary Studies

Mark Bruhn, *Cognition, Literature and History*, co-edited with Don R. Wehrs. Routledge, 2014.

Liane Gabora, *Quantum Structures in Cognitive and Social Science*, co-edited with Diederik Aerts, Jan Broekaert, and Sandro Sozzo. Frontiers Psychology Research Topics, 2016.

Patrick Colm Hogan, *Literature and Emotion.* Routledge, 2018.

Karin Kukkonen, *Probability Designs: Literature and Predictive Processing.* Oxford UP, 2019.

Paula Leverage, *Theory of Mind and Literature,* co-edited with Jennifer Marston William, Howard Mancing and Richard Schweickert. Purdue UP, 2011.

Keith Oatley, *Our Minds, Our Selves: A Brief History of Psychology.* Princeton UP, 2018.

Pierre-Louis Patoine, *Corps/Texte: Pour une théorie de la lecture empathique.* ENS éditions, 2015.

Deborah Prentice, *Social Neuroscience: Toward Understanding the Underpinnings of the Social Mind*, co-edited with Alexander Todorov and Susan Fiske. Oxford UP, 2011.

Donovan O. Schaefer, *The Evolution of Affect Theory.* Cambridge UP, 2019.

Gabrielle Starr, *Feeling Beauty: The Neuroscience of Aesthetic Experience.* MIT Press, 2013.

Jason Tougaw, *The Elusive Brain: Literary Experiments in the Age of Neuroscience.* Yale UP, 2018.

Emily Troscianko, *Cognitive Literary Science: Dialogues Between Literature and Cognition*, co-edited with Michael Burke. Oxford UP, 2017.

Don R. Wehrs, *The Palgrave Handbook of Affect Studies and Textual Criticism*, co-edited with Thomas Blake. Palgrave, 2017.

Australian Literary Studies

Jan Alber, *Unnatural Narrative: Impossible Worlds in Fiction and Drama.* Nebraska UP, 2016.

Craig Batty, *The Doctoral Experience: Student Stories From the Creative Arts and Humanities*, co-edited with Donna Lee Brien, Elizabeth Ellison, and Alison Owens. Palgrave, 2020.

Nicholas Birns, *Contemporary Australian Literature: A World Not Yet Dead.* Sydney UP, 2015.

David Carter, *Australian Books and Authors in the American Marketplace: 1840s-1940s*, written with Roger Osborne. Sydney UP, 2018.

Marcelle Freiman, *White Lines (Vertical).* Hybrid Publishers, 2010.

Jessica Gildersleeve (Editor), *The Routledge Companion to Australian Literature.* Routledge, 2020.

Dennis Haskell, *Attuned to Alien Moonlight: The Poetry of Bruce Dawe.* Queensland UP, 2002.

Graham Huggan, *Australian Literature: Postcolonial, Racism, Transnationalism.* Oxford UP, 2007.

Tony Hughes D'Aeth, *Like Nothing on This Earth: A Literary History of the Wheatbelt* (U Western Australia Publishing, 2017.

Nicholas Jose (Editor), *The Literature of Australia: An Anthology.* W.W. Norton, 2009.

Christopher Ringrose, *New Soundings in Postcolonial Writing: Critical and Creative Contours*, co-edited with Janet Wilson. Rodopi, 2016.

Geoff Rodoreda, *The Mabo Turn in Australian Fiction.* Peter Lang, 2018.

John Stephens, *Language and Ideology in Children's Fiction.* Longman, 1992.

1 Cognitive Australian Literary Studies and the Creation of New Heuristic Constellations[1]

Jean-François Vernay

Introduction

Australian literary studies started to show the first encouraging signs of influence by cognitive literary studies in the early 2000s, a decade or so after the cognitive turn made its mark on American scholarly publishing. The last, particularly prolific years (2013–2021), have been instrumental in turning cognitive Australian literary studies from an emerging trend into an ever-expanding, ripening discipline which now begs for a timely synoptic survey.

While a much larger number of Australian scholars have been seeking convergence between cognitivism and the humanities at large, this chapter will restrict the scope of discussion to *cognitive* Australian literary studies, namely writers dealing with Australian literary studies enhanced by cognitive approaches. It will therefore exclude *Australian* cognitive literary studies – an even more inclusive category which would comprise all Australian scholars taking a vested interest in cognitive literary studies.

After contextualizing cognitive Australian literary studies globally and defining them, this article will survey the field of cognitive-inspired Australian fiction and non-fiction and assess how this new direction in contemporary Australian criticism might create promising overtures in the Australian humanities.

Cognitive Australian Literary Studies: Genesis, Definition, and Context

While the cognitive turn was heralded by a spate of seminal publications released in the United States from the early 1990s, such as Mark Turner's *Reading Minds: The Study of English in the Age of Cognitive Science* (1991) and Marie-Laure Ryan's *Possible Worlds,*

Artificial Intelligence, and Narrative Theory (1991), the earliest book-length theoretical work in cognitive literary studies was Reuven Tsur's short treatise entitled *What Is Cognitive Poetics?* (1983). Yet the very definition of this cutting-edge field remains elusive: an interdisciplinary approach, no consonance of paradigms, an inspiration from cognitive science research, a concern for issues in literary studies blended with neurological insights, the use of multiple prisms, and a certain overcautiousness seem to be the chief characteristics defining this ever-broadening category. The pervasive over-cautiousness in the field is a direct consequence of scant knowledge of the brain and its processes, insufficient research in cognitive science focusing on fiction, the technological limitations in brain-imaging techniques, the difficulty of obtaining cut-and-dried findings, not to mention some form of political correctness due to the fact that very few scholars are at ease with discussing the possibility of brain-related gender differences.

Though all these major traits can easily be discerned, providing an all-encompassing definition of a field known for its sheer heterogeneity may prove difficult, but I may venture one. Cognitive literary studies could be summarized as *a cluster of various literary criticism-related disciplines forming a broad-based trend which draws on the findings of cognitive science to sharpen their psychological understanding of literature by exploring the mental processes at work in the creative minds of writers and readers*. As a contemporary of postmodernism, this ground-breaking conception of literature is revelatory in its attempt to fine-tune a scientific-cum-anthropological perception of fiction by delving into the complexities of the various mental processes it involves. Although conducive to interdisciplinary convergence, the pollination of two highly interdisciplinary fields like cognitive science and literary studies was bound to proliferate into a great many neighboring disciplines, a complex constellation of subsets which is far from forming a unified research field.

It is however possible to divide cognitive literary studies into five major epistemologically related, though disparate, strains which often feed into one another: cognitive literary history (which this present chapter typifies); evolutionary literary criticism (ranging from bio-cultural approaches to Darwinian literary studies); neuro lit crit (a neurologizing approach to literature branching out into neuroesthetics which covers mainly art, esthetics, and the brain); cognitively informed preexisting theories (encompassing cognitive poetics, cognitive rhetoric, cognitive narratology, cognitive stylistics, cognitive ecocriticism, cognitive queer studies, cognitive postcolonial studies, *inter alia*); and affective literary theory.

Following this broader definition, cognitive Australian literary studies could therefore be defined as literary scholarship concerned with the examination of Australian literature from any of the above-mentioned strains, or even from a blend of any of them. To be sure, it may be problematic to identify whether some of the scholarship qualifies for this category or not. Ultimately, this is a matter of personal appreciation, as there is no official way to indicate how much these studies should borrow from cognitive science or discuss Australian literature to be labeled *cognitive* Australian literary criticism. Having said this, the primary sources listed in these academic discussions should give a fair idea of their ideological orientation and interest in Australian culture. For instance, Anthony Uhlmann's "Where Literary Studies Is, and What It Does" (2013) is no exegesis of Australian literature per se, yet it discusses cognitive poetics in relation to the teaching of English literatures, which de facto includes Australian literature. However, his very brief discussion of cognitive poetics and his sole reference to cognitive neuroscience (the oft-cited 2013 David Comer Kidd and Emanuele Castano theory of mind experiment which has been successfully replicated by the same team and two others since 2018) could potentially be seen as too minimal for his article to be listed in the bibliography of cognitive Australian literary studies I have compiled at the end of *The Rise of the Australian Neurohumanities.*

Among the five main strains of cognitive literary studies, affective literary theory is arguably the most dynamic one in Australia as it has benefitted from the multifarious activities of an impressive seven-year collegial project (2011–2018) funded by the Australian Research Council. The generous grant has enabled the establishment of a Center for the History of Emotions through five university nodes in almost all states (South Australia, New South Wales, Victoria, Queensland, and Western Australia) along with a half-yearly refereed journal – *Emotions: History, Culture, Society* (2017–ongoing) – published under the auspices of the Society for the History of Emotions, founded in 2016. However, to date, perhaps because of the journal's multidisciplinary nature, editors Kartie Barclay, Andrew Lynch, and Giovanni Tarantino have only included one article dealing with Australian literary studies (McAlister) over the release of eight issues. Yet, to be fair, Jody McAlister's article does not really engage with affect studies per se and takes a more thematic approach to emotions in colonial romances. A quick survey of the bibliography included at the end of this volume should conveniently give a bird's eye view of progress made in this emergent field, which has been particularly prolific over the past two decades. As Emmett Stinson has it, "The state of literary criticism in Australia resists any easy summary, because it has far too many fields and subfields to present a unified object" (125). Yet, we could argue that cognitive Australian literary studies shares the interdisciplinarity and methodological methods of cultural studies to a certain degree. At the dawn of the twenty-first century, clusters of Australian cognitive literary studies began to emerge loosely within a few Australian universities – such as Macquarie University in Sydney, or Deakin University and Swinburne University in Melbourne – without setting up a proper Center for NeuroHumanities such as the kind you will find at Purdue University, in the United States, or without founding an Association of Cognitive Poetics similar to the Chinese one which came into existence in 2013. As a result, one might argue that because of this lack of structuring into a close-knit community of scholars aiming at concerted effort, cognitive Australian literary studies has had a slow emergence and is still making progress toward becoming a strong and consolidated field to be reckoned with.

Surveying the Field of Cognitive-Inspired Fiction and Non-Fiction

In comparison with American and British writers, a cluster of whom have been credited for contributing to the rise of the "neuronovel," precious few Australian authors have been credited with their works under this label, even though a few of them are fascinated by the neuroscience of creative writing. To some extent, Sue Woolfe and Colleen McCullough might be the only Australian authors who could be associated with this group of neuronovelists chiefly composed of American writers such as Jonathan Lethem, Nancy Huston, Siri Hustvedt, Richard Powers, and John Wray, and British representatives such as Ned Beauman, Ian McEwan, and Mark Haddon. A few Australian authors have even had the privilege of a professional background in neuroscience, which has fed into their creative writings. The two most prominent examples that come to mind are bestselling novelist Colleen McCullough, who taught in the Department of Neurology at the Yale Medical School in Connecticut before publishing *On, Off* (2005) some three decades later, and poet Ian Gibbins, professor of anatomy at Flinders University (Adelaide), also a neuroscientist until he retired in 2014. Some of his poetry, often inspired by Dadaism and Surrealism, is substantially informed by neuroscience such as "Lessons in neuroscience." The six mini lessons, respectively, deal with phantom limbs, the vestibular system of balance in the inner ear, the solitary tract known for processing visceral sensations, the trigeminal nerve chiefly responsible for sensation in the face, gate control theory that accounts for pain sensation not being able to access the central nervous system, and the almond-shaped amygdala that plays a central role in the processing of emotions such as fear and pleasure. The "Entorhinal" poem focuses on spatial memory and path finding, while "Cataplexy" is an esthetic interpretation of the eponymous neurological condition. "No Glutamate" is based on one of Ian Gibbins's scholarly papers about nerve fibers that transmit painful stimuli (Morris).

Although their subject matter cannot be labeled as neurofiction, many contemporary Australian novels, as say, in crime fiction (see Newton), are highly conducive to research in cognitive Australian literary studies. The study of what I call *neurodivergence fiction* also falls squarely in the remit of this innovative field. For instance, Sue Woolfe's *The Secret Cure* (2003) and Graeme Simsion's *The Rosie Project* (2013) and its sequels are prime material for cognitive criticism, not to mention Toni Jordan's *Addition* (2008), which has already been discussed in terms of cognitive disability for its attention to obsessive-compulsive disorder (Robertson). It should be added that these cultural representations of characters afflicted by mental disorders are instrumental in helping empathizing neurotypical readers come to a better understanding of cognitive difference. Some genres whose narratives involve the (sometimes dysfunctional) workings of the mind, such as Philip Salom's second novel entitled *Toccata and Rain* (2004), seem to be particularly suited to the cognitivist study of literature. At the core of the narrator's account lie the complexities of a pathology known as fugue amnesia or dissociative fugue. To resist split, Brian (also known as Simon) has to overwrite himself like a "human palimpsest," with one story superseding another. Salom has pursued the interrelated themes of eccentricities and vulnerabilities in *The Returns* (2019) with Elizabeth, one of the main characters, who suffers from prosopagnosia — face blindness. Peter Kocan's total institution novellas, *The Treatment* (1980) and *The Cure* (1983), also address neurodivergence as a central theme. Total institution fiction is defined as literature concerned with characters confined to reclusion in total institutions and living in very close quarters with other inmates, all of whom are placed under one supervising and all-powerful authority that is the keystone to an administratively structured organization (see Vernay, "The Art of Penning The March Hare In").

Other genres conducive to the cognitivist study of literature include books in which the main action is set in a neuroscientific environment or based on neural technology, as exemplified by Colleen McCullough's *On, Off* and Angela Meyer's *A Superior Spectre* (2018). Psychological narratives like Peter Goldsworthy's *Three Dog Night* (2003) and virtually any of Patrick White's novels, as well as narratives underpinned by or dealing with emotions (such as romance novels or works by John M. Coetzee, Christos Tsiolkas, Peter Carey, to mention a few), science and speculative fiction tapping into the unexploited possibilities of the mind typified by Greg Egan's *Quarantine* (1992) and *Teranesia* (1999) should all be included here.

True accounts of neurological damage and neuroplastic recovery as in the consequences of David Roland's stroke in *How I Rescued My Brain* (2014) are choice material for cognitive Australian literary studies. Whether caused by a car accident, as recounted in Christine Bryden's *Unlocking My Brain: Through the Labyrinth of Acquired Brain Injury* (2014) and Sarah Brooker's *My Lucky Stroke* (2020), or by a horse riding fall (see Sarah Vallance), traumatic brain injuries often prompt the victims to process their ghastly life-changing event into restorative memoirs through a preliminary phase of lucid introspective journaling that is later edited into a book. In a similar vein, trauma accounts such as Meer Atkinson's *Traumata* (2018) and mental health memoirs like Nicola Redhouse's *Unlike the Heart: A Memoir of Brain and Mind* (2019) on postpartum anxiety disorder are indicative of the strong cultural influence neuroscience has in Australian contemporary society.

More generally, if we are to construe reader reception as a meeting of two minds, that of the writer who produces the text and that of the reader who consumes it, then cognitive Australian literary studies would find its usefulness in analyzing any work of literature. This would go a long way toward explaining why Australian children's literature has received a great deal of critical attention in this field, even though juvenile fiction is not particularly known for being concerned with brain-related issues.

John Stephens is to be credited with being the first Australian scholar to have published his work in the field of cognitive Australian literary studies. His writings on textual patterning in Australian children's literature draw substantially on schema theory in relation to social cognition. Indeed, the bulk of Australian literary research inspired by cognitive literary criticism between 2002 and 2021 falls into five categories: cognitive readings of Australian literary works (see Britten, Pettitt, Rubik, Stephens); creativity-focused research for which *TEXT* and *Axon* journals are the most sought-after publishing outlets (see Brophy, Prendergast, Takolander, Woolfe); body-related investigations (see Giles, Spencer); brain-inspired studies (see Fitzpatrick, Hayles, Newton, Robertson); and writings informed by affect theory (see Barnett and Douglas, Farrell, Gildersleeve, Heister, McAlister, Mudiyanselage, Stasny, Stephens, Thomas). Since cognitive literary studies are particularly adept at disclosing the invisible, namely not so much what lies within the porous text (the subtext) as what happens in the writer's or reader's brain, it makes sense that a great deal of Australian research has focused on how neuroscience can shed light on creativity. Unsurprisingly, the major contributors to the field are the writers straddling creative writing and scholarship: poets Maria Takolander and Kevin Brophy, and novelists Sue Woolfe and Julia Prendergast, have been spearheading this Australian research in neurocreativity.

In *The Mystery of The Cleaning Lady: A Writer Looks at Creativity and Neuroscience* (2007), Woolfe takes a rare insider's perspective into creativity by examining in turn a series of engaging and thematically connected topics: literary inspiration and the creative mood, the agency and vivacity of the creative imagination, the interaction of thoughts and images, the transmission of information, emotional involvement and empathy, the creative personality, synesthesia and metaphor-building, and the defocusing of the mind. It was inspired by Christopher David Stevens's doctoral dissertation in psychology, for which he interviewed "seven successful Australian fiction writers about their insights" (1) without disclosing their names. Woolfe, who has confessed to have taken part in this experiment, also elaborates on George Kelly's discussion of two main forms of thinking. According to this American psychologist, one is to distinguish between "'tight' construing (or secondary-process thinking) and 'loose' construing (or primary-process thinking)," in which literary creativity seems to blossom (Woolfe 91). Loose construing therefore involves putting our capacity to anticipate and predict outcomes on hold, thus paving the way to a daydreaming mode in which "[j]udgements are suspended. Self-consciousness and self-censorship are minimized. People often talk of experiencing an altered sense of self, with a loss of the sense of time and place and a blurring of self and others, and self and the world" (92). Such cutting-edge perspectives on literature and its creative minds are bound to afford "overtures" (Alder and Gross 195) or "openings" (Cave 31) in a long-existing field which Australian literary historiography dates back to 1856 (with the publication of Frederick Sinnett's essay, "The Fiction Fields of Australia"). It is not hard to see how cognitive Australian literary studies can shed light on hitherto neglected aspects of Australian literature all the while shrewdly renewing its academic approaches and discourse.

A Simmering Field Affording Overtures in the Humanities

Within the last three decades, cognitive literary studies have gradually been making their mark on the international publishing arena with a growing number of theoretical works blending scientific approaches with literary theory, a trend which can be seen as narrowing the divide between, as Charles Percy Snow terms it, "The Two Cultures." In an irrepressible bout of optimism, this slowly emerging current can even be taken to be the missing link, if not the ideal interface, between science and the humanities. Yet, this new conceptual approach blending humanistic and scientific inquiry is strikingly reminiscent of countless methods of critical analysis which have more or less involved a desire to establish a literary science (Vernay 3–4).

Giving a new direction to Australian literary criticism under the sway of cognitivism will encourage Australianists to avail themselves of scientific concepts and of substantial knowledge of the human anatomy and physiology at large. They will also be required to take an inventory of the neurobabble that will generate fresh outlooks on Australian literature, understood both as an archive and a practice. With such daunting tasks on the literary agenda, this somewhat controversial new field is bound to meet a great deal of resistance in mainstream academia, given that it may estrange more traditional literary critics from cognitive literary studies.

The evidence that some expected form of misoneism is already at work can hardly be gainsaid if one is to briefly analyze the various types of editors and publishers running articles by cognitive literary scholars. A giveaway might be detected in the fact that the overwhelming majority of the essays dealing with Australian fiction has been published outside the classical leading outlets renowned for promoting Australian literary studies, with the exception of Meg Mundell's "Crafting 'Literary Sense of Place': The Generative Work of Literary Place-Making" (2018) and Victoria Reeve's "Emotion and Narratives of Heartland: Kim Scott's *Benang* and Peter Carey's *Jack Maggs*" (2013) which discusses the interaction dynamics of narrative and emotions. Both articles were published in the *Journal of the Association for the Study of Australian Literature (JASAL)*. As to all the other essays, rather than appearing in *Australian Literary Studies*, *LINQ* (which has now been absorbed by *eTropic*), *Meanjin*, *Overland*, *Quadrant*, *Southerly*, or *Westerly*, they have been published in Australian general journals, whether discipline-specific like *Papers: Explorations into Children's Literature*, *TEXT*, *Aurealis*, and *Axon*, or multidisciplinary like *Australian Humanities Review* and *Australasian Journal of Popular Culture*. The rest of the scholarship has appeared in international journals (*Antipodes*, *International Research in Children's Literature*, *Media Tropes*, *New Writing: The International Journal for the Practice and Theory of Creative Writing*, and *European Journal of English Studies*), or multi-chapter works such as single-author monographs, edited volumes, and conference proceedings.

The persistent push in Australian universities for interdisciplinary necessity is conducive to the flourishing of this discipline which could increase student cohorts and broaden audiences while giving graduates more versatility to their profiles. What could be quickly dismissed as an umpteenth interdisciplinary approach may even hold the key to helping Australian scholars under institutional pressure to remain cutting edge in their research activity. There is no doubt that retrofitting literary criticism with scientific concepts will create overtures and renew the paraphernalia of critical tools, both of which will revitalize Australian literary studies.

At the intersection of literary studies and cognitive science, literary topics such as imagination, realistic depiction, imagery and figures of speech, literary comprehension and reception, identification, the paratext, emotions, fiction reading – in short, "language, mental acts and linguistic artefacts" (Richardson and Steen 1) – are now examined under close scrutiny through the lens of science and reassessed in a more accurate way, which essentially means in accordance with human physiology. This new vision of literature, of its artifacts and their mental processing, provides a refreshing perspective and added value to Australian literary studies. As Michael Burke and Emily T. Troscianko advocate,

> There are many obvious ways in which the cognitive sciences [...] have the potential to enrich literary studies. These disciplines can make substantial contributions to how literary scholars understand processes of textual creation and reception, as well as textually evoked cognition. (141)

Cognitive Australian literary studies – very much like cultural studies, which also emerged at a time of crisis in the humanities and was then disparaged in its early phase (see Hall) – could potentially be hailed as widening the scope of the literary issues that narratives generate and granting the Australian literary canon more scope and flexibility. Neurocognitive readings of Australian literature make it possible for scholars to create new heuristic constellations by discussing neglected aspects of literature, such as narrative impact on readers, about which classic close readings of literary texts can only speculate. One example among many is Margarete Rubik's article on Peter Carey's short fiction, which testifies to the fresh insight that a cognitive perspective can bring to particular works of Australian fiction. "Provocative and Unforgettable: Peter Carey's Short Fiction" is a telling example of how to incorporate cognitive poetics into a classical literary analysis combining close readings of selected short stories and a broader view of the writer's narrative techniques. Margarete Rubik cogently explains how "Carey's consummate manipulation of cognitive schemata and clashing cognitive frames [...] prevents closure and leaves the reader puzzling for an interpretation" (169). Giving us insight into how Carey's short fiction tends to climax in destabilizing images that deny readers cognitive closure is somewhat more enlightening than just stating that the writer has a talent for writing bizarre short stories which readers find unsettling.

If I were to take a more personal example from my forthcoming monograph, *Neurocognitive Interpretations of Australian Literature: Criticism in the Age of Neuroawareness*, I would mention my take on the humorous *Rosie* trilogy written by Graeme Simsion and his editorial collaborators. *The Rosie Project* (2013) and its two sequels articulate the complex interactive relationship between Aspergic difference, cultural representations, and the rhetorics of disability. While these Australian high-functioning ASD novels have not been written by a neurodivergent writer, its core treatment of neurodivergence is obviously conducive to neurocognitive readings of literature. Using the *Rosie* trilogy as a case study, I demonstrate in this book chapter how the literary representation of a neurodivergent mind style translates into a distinctive literary style and the creation of a new subset of fiction.

Cognitive Australian literary studies aim to guide readers through the complexities underlying the creation, comprehension, consumption, and interpretation of fiction while renewing the tradition of Australian literary criticism by redefining its concepts, goals, and priorities. By coloring the language of Australian literary criticism with cognitive methodology or explanatory frameworks and by affording a shift of angle which reconfigures the whole field of literary studies, cognitive Australian literary studies is on its way to finding its pertinence in our increasingly brain-based society. The interpenetration of cognitive science and Australian literary studies could be construed as the logical outcome of a field eager to "reinvigorate the study of Australian literature both locally and internationally." However, to date, it is worth noting that the Sydney Studies in Australian Literature series, which overtly nurtures this ambition, has not yet published a monograph informed by cognitive literary studies. Rather, the 12 titles that have been issued so far have adopted mainstream approaches to Australian literary criticism.

Conclusion

This introductory chapter drawing on cognitive literary history methodology has retraced the genesis and current context of cognitive Australian literary studies, whose interdisciplinary nature is expected to facilitate the engagement of Australian humanities and mind sciences in a fruitful dialog. Indeed, while literature has the capacity to give scientific knowledge an extension through active imaginative engagement, science also has the ability to extend our understanding of literature and prevent the intellectual breathlessness which might ensue from a lack of interdisciplinarity. Not only has this cross-fertilization of ideas the potential to bring new insights to the study of Australian literature, but it could also help narrow the divide between science and literature, often presented as rival disciplines.

The current scholarship in cognitive Australian literary criticism comes across as isolated yet brave endeavors to bridge the gap between Australian literature and cutting-edge forms of literary reception. The organization of this emergent domain in clusters of research centers in which cognitive Australian literary critics could participate in more concerted action will be a decisive factor for this field to become a new direction in contemporary Australian criticism.

Note

1 This chapter is an updated and expanded version of a commissioned chapter entitled "Towards a New Direction in Contemporary Criticism: Cognitive Australian Literary Studies," which appeared in Jessica Gildersleeve (ed.), *The Routledge Companion to Australian Literature* (London/New York: Routledge, 2020), 116–122. The bibliography of the scholars whose work is mentioned in passing is available in the final section of this volume: *Cognitive Australian Literary Studies: A Selective Bibliography.*

Works Cited

Alder, Hans, and Sabine Gross. "Adjusting the Frame: Comments on Cognitivism and Literature." *Poetics Today*, vol. 23, no. 2, 2002, pp. 195–220.

Brophy, Kevin. *Patterns of Creativity. Investigations into the Sources and Methods of Creativity*. Rodopi, 2009.

Burke, Michael, and Emily T. Troscianko. "Mind, Brain and Literature: A Dialogue on What the Humanities Might Offer the Cognitive Sciences." *Journal of Literary Semantics*, vol. 42, no. 2, 2013, pp. 141–148.

Cave, Terence. *Thinking with Literature: Towards a Cognitive Criticism*. Oxford UP, 2016.

Hall, Stuart. "The Emergence of Cultural Studies and the Crisis of the Humanities." *October*, vol. 53, 1990, pp. 11–23.

Kidd, David Comer, and Emanuele Castano. "Reading Literary Fiction and Theory of Mind: Three Preregistered Replications and Extensions of Kidd and Castano (2013)." *Social and Psychological and Personality Science*, vol. 10, no. 4, 20 June 2018, pp. 522–531.

Kidd, David Comer, and Emanuele Castano. "Reading Literary Fiction Improves Theory of Mind." *Science*, vol. 342, 18 October 2013, pp. 377–380.

McAlister, Jody. "'Feelings Like the Women in Books': Declarations of Love in Australian Romance Novels, 1859–1891." *Emotions: History, Culture, Society*, vol. 2, no. 1, 2018, pp. 91–112.

Morris, Judy, Peter Koenig, Toshihiko Shimizu, Philip Jobling, and Ian Gibbins. "Most Peptide-containing Sensory Neurons Lack Proteins for Exocytotic Release and Vesicular Transport of Glutamate." *Journal of Comparative Neurology*, vol. 483, 2005, pp. 1–16.

Mundell, Meg. "Crafting 'Literary Sense of Place': The Generative Work of Literary Place-Making." *JASAL*, vol. 18, no. 1, 2018, https://openjournals.library.sydney.edu.au/index.php/JASAL/article/viewFile/12375/11762

Prendergast, Julia. "Grinding the Moor – Ideasthesia and Narrative." *New Writing*, vol. 15, no. 4, 2018, pp. 416–432.

Prendergast, Julia. "Narrative and the Unthought Known: The Immaterial Intelligence of Form." *TEXT*, vol. 23, no. 1, 2019, https://www.textjournal.com.au/april19/prendergast.htm.

Reeve, Victoria. "Emotion and Narratives of Heartland: Kim Scott's *Benang* and Peter Carey's *Jack Maggs*." *JASAL*, vol. 12, no. 3, 2013, pp. 1–11, https://openjournals.library.sydney.edu.au/index.php/JASAL/article/view/9830/9718.

Richardson, Alan, and Francis F. Steen. "Literature and the Cognitive Revolution: An Introduction." *Poetics Today*, vol. 23, no. 1, 2002, pp. 1–8.

Robertson, Rachel. "'Driven by Tens': Obsession and Cognitive Difference in Toni Jordan's Romantic Comedy *Addition*." *Australasian Journal of Popular Culture*, vol. 3, no. 3, 2014, pp. 311–320.

Rubik, Margarete. "Provocative and Unforgettable: Peter Carey's Short Fiction." *European Journal of English Studies*, vol. 9, no. 2, 2005, pp. 169–184.

Snow, Charles Percy. *The Two Cultures: And a Second Look*. Cambridge UP, 1959.

Stevens, Christopher David. *Crooked Paths to Insight: The Pragmatic of Loose and Tight Construing*. Unpublished PhD diss. University of Wollongong, 1999.

Stinson, Emmett. "Literary Criticism in Australia." *The Routledge Companion to Australian Literature*, edited by Jessica Gildersleeve. Routledge, 2020, pp. 125–133.

Uhlmann, Anthony. "Where Literary Studies Is, and What It Does." *Australian Literary Studies*, vol. 28, no. 1-2, 2013, pp. 98–110.

Vernay, Jean-François. "The Art of Penning the March Hare In: The Treatment of Insanity in Australian Total Institution Fiction." *AUMLA*, vol. 118, 2012, pp. 87–103.

Vernay, Jean-François. *The Seduction of Fiction: A Plea for Putting Emotions Back into Literary Interpretation*. Palgrave, 2016.

Vernay, Jean-François. *Neurocognitive Interpretations of Australian Literature: Criticism in the Age of Neuroawareness*. Routledge, 2021.

Woolfe, Sue. *The Mystery of The Cleaning Lady: A Writer Looks at Creativity and Neuroscience*. U Western Australia Publishing, 2007.

2 Narrative Empathy in Contemporary Australian Multiperspectival Novels: Cognitive Readings of Christos Tsiolkas's *The Slap* and Gail Jones's *Five Bells*[1]

Lukas Klik

Introduction

In recent years, hardly any field within literary studies has been un-affected by the rise and proliferation of cognitive studies. This en-thusiasm for the insights of cognitive studies, as Lisa Zunshine suggests, is currently leading to the development of "a broad variety of paradigms and approaches" (3) within literary studies. My own ap-proach taken in this essay is one informed by cognitive narratology. In accordance with the main aim of Cognitive Literary Studies, as pointed out by Jean-François Vernay, this chapter is guided by the interest "in disclosing the invisible, namely not so much what lies within the porous text (i.e. the subtext) as what happens in the writer's or reader's head" (113). More precisely, I am interested in the issue of narrative empathy, a discussion that has been fueled in particular by the works of Suzanne Keen and that David Herman deems one of the "[e]mergent [t]rends" (35) in cognitive narratology.

In what follows, I focus on contemporary Australian multi-perspectival novels. By "multiperspectival novels," I understand texts in which the reader accesses the storyworld through the multiple viewpoints of different focalizers. In particular, I am interested in how these texts may privilege some perspectives over others by prompting readers to feel empathy with some focalizers rather than others. In this context, I argue that narrative empathy as a result of a text's multi-perspectivity is more likely to arise if the narrative exacerbates conflict between focalizers. Here, I discuss Christos Tsiolkas's *The Slap* (2008) and Gail Jones's *Five Bells* (2011), the latter of which I approach from a trauma studies perspective, to show how they differ in the ways in which they trigger narrative empathy. Both texts respond to demographic changes within Australia and present an increasingly multicultural nation. Besides discussing the relationship between narrative empathy and multiperspectivity, this chapter, then, also addresses how readerly empathy in literature may be a means to foster greater understanding for a diversifying society, especially but not only in the Australian context.

Theoretical Considerations: Multiperspectivity and Narrative Empathy

Multiperspectivity is a notoriously difficult term to define. In the context of my chapter, however, I understand multiperspectivity, in line with Marcus Hartner, as "a mode of storytelling in which multiple and often discrepant viewpoints are employed for the presentation and evaluation of a story and its storyworld" (Hartner 353). For Birgit Neumann and Ansgar Nünning, multiperspectival narratives include either various narrators, various focalizing instances, or various textual genres, such as "letters or newspaper articles" (Neumann and Nünning 102). For my purposes, only the second aspect is of interest, since the multiperspectivity of *The Slap* and *Five Bells* is the result of a variety of different focalizing instances that operate independently of the act of narration.[2] From a narratological point of view, both texts are heterodiegetic narratives with shifting internal focalization. There are, in other words, multiple focalizers that present varying glimpses of the storyworld.

As literary characters, focalizers may trigger readers to feel empathy with them. According to Suzanne Keen, narrative empathy can be defined as the "vicarious, spontaneous sharing of affect" (*Novel* 4), more specifically "the sharing of feeling and perspective-taking induced by reading, viewing, hearing, or imagining narratives of another's situation and condition" ("Narrative Empathy" 521). Importantly, Keen insists upon the contemporary differentiation between empathy and sympathy, a distinction that everyday discourse often fails to make.[3] In contrast to sympathy, which manifests itself as "feelings *for* another" (Keen, *Novel* 5), empathy enables readers to experience "the *same* feeling" (Keen, "Empathy Studies" 130) as a particular character. For Roy Sommer, empathy is "an effect largely created by the text itself, the product of dramaturgical strategies and narrative techniques" (159). Indeed, as I will discuss below, it stands to reason that certain textual features may be more inclined to generate empathy within readers than others. At the same time, however, a strict mapping of textual elements and their effects is, of course, impossible. After all, not everyone is triggered emotionally by the same components of a text and, even more generally, research has shown that some individuals have a stronger tendency to empathize than others (Keen, *Novel* 10). Empathy is, then, best understood as a product of the reading process that may, though need not necessarily, be triggered by certain textual features, but which is eventually determined by the individual reader's subjectivity.

Besides the individual disposition of readers, there are also plot-related aspects as well as textual features that may play a role in generating narrative empathy. Focusing on the first, Fritz Breithaupt defines empathy as the effect that arises when an observer of a conflict between at least two individuals takes side with one of them (152–153). For him, this includes perspective-taking (Breithaupt 157). Empathy, then, necessarily involves three participants or more, but perhaps, considering how literature can also trigger empathic reactions for characters that are in conflict with themselves, it is more accurate to say that for empathy to come about, there must be at least three different, conflicting worldviews present. In this sense, empathy results from this side-taking, though Breithaupt similarly concedes that it – at least partially – also determines it in the first place (156–157). In other words, we feel with someone because we have decided to take sides with her/him (see also Serino et al.), though this decision has also been influenced by our ability to feel empathy with her/him. For my purposes here, such an understanding of empathy is helpful, since it can explain the different degrees to which narrative empathy operates in the novels under discussion. In terms of textual features and methods that may generate narrative empathy, *"character identification"* and *"narrative situation"* (Keen, *Novel* 93)[4] seem to be prominent aspects. With regard to character identification, scholars have argued that readers particularly respond to those texts that describe aspects with which they are familiar (Keen, *Novel* 94). Familiarity as the basis for an emotional response can take different forms, though. Patrick Colm Hogan distinguishes between "categorical empathy" and "situational empathy." While the first describes a reader's empathy based on her/his group affiliation, the latter poses that readers are more likely to experience empathy for plot-related aspects, if they themselves have encountered similar situations as those described in the narratives (Hogan 135–136; Keen, *Novel* 80).

Yet, while familiarity may facilitate empathic responses, one can also feel for others who are radically different. C. Daniel Batson and Nadia Y. Ahmad, for instance, have noted the potential of empathy to "help improve intergroup attitudes and relations," in particular when it involves "the increased awareness of the pressures faced by members of an out-group that an imagine-self perspective can provide" (Batson and Ahmad 173). It is exactly here that the capacity of narrative empathy to promote diversity comes in. After all, fiction can make readers conscious of the hardships of marginalized groups, especially, though not exclusively, when characters of "out-group[s]" act as focalizers and readers hence take up "an imagine-self perspective" through their eyes. At this point, it is necessary to consider the positions of authors, too, since writers can employ empathy strategically in order to meet certain aims. In this regard, Keen distinguishes three forms of "[s]trategic empathy" (*Novel* 142). It can be "*bounded*," if its goal is that only members of a particular group respond empathically; "*ambassadorial*," if only a "chosen" few should feel with the group; or "*broadcast*," if everyone should "feel with members of a group" in that the text stresses what all humans have in common (Keen, *Novel* 142).

In terms of narrative situations that can help generate such an effect, scholars have often noted the potential of "an internal perspective" (Keen, *Novel* 96), be it in the form of homodiegetic narration or heterodiegetic narration with internal focalization. However, perhaps to the great disappointment of many narratologists, research has shown that narrative situation may in fact play a less significant role in narrative empathy than often assumed. The results of Willie van Peer and Henk Pander Maat's empirical study, for instance, indicate that its effect is rather limited (152). Despite these results, Peer and Pander Maat argue that it would be incorrect to claim that it has no importance whatsoever. They suggest that "[i]t would seem that effects of point of view are not independent of a story's subject matter. More particularly, its effects will be more directly felt to the degree that a conflict between main characters exists or arises in the course of the story" (Peer and Pander Maat 152). Here, they make an important point in that they connect Breithaupt's plot-oriented approach to empathy with considerations of textual features creating empathy. As already noted, this link is especially vital for my argument in that, following Peer and Pander Maat and Breithaupt, I suggest that a narrative's multiperspectivity can generate empathy particularly if the narrative foregrounds conflict. In the following, I want to substantiate this argument in my textual readings by comparing how narrative empathy operates differently in a multiperspectival novel exacerbating conflict between characters, such as *The Slap*, and one not doing so, such as *Five Bells*.

Conflict, Multiperspectivity, and Narrative Empathy in Christos Tsiolkas's *The Slap* (2008)

If, as Breithaupt has suggested, empathy is the result of side-taking in a conflict between at least three participants, or, as I have phrased it, three clearly distinguishable, conflicting worldviews, *The Slap* (2008) lends itself as a good case in point to describe how narrative empathy operates. Set in a community of family members and friends in the suburbs of Melbourne, Tsiolkas's novel revolves around the conflicts between the eight focalizers that arise when at the beginning of the narrative a man slaps a friend's child, supposedly under the assumption that the child was about to hurt his own son. Soon, fractures between the characters develop when the parents of the child sue the perpetrator unsuccessfully and the novel's interest in diversity becomes evident.

Indeed, as many critics have argued, difference is at the heart of the novel (Dunlop 7; McCann 100; Treagus 9). The novel's focalizing characters are immensely varied in terms of gender, ethnicity, class, sexuality, or age. Through this large number of highly diverse character-focalizers with their various intersecting identity categories, the potential for categorical empathy is perhaps greater in *The Slap* than in *Five Bells*. While aged readers may feel with Manolis, the oldest focalizer of the novel, more easily than with other characters, an LGBTQ reader may more readily empathize with Richie, the gay teenager who has not yet come out of the closet and who acts as the novel's final focalizer. This is, then, a typical example of the relation between identification and empathy.

Although categorical empathy may be particularly strong in *The Slap*, it is in the interpretation of the eponymous slap (Tsiolkas 40) that the novel is able to generate empathy most strongly. The various characters react quite differently to the initial incident. While some defend the behavior of Harry, the perpetrator of the slap, mainly, though not exclusively, due to their family ties to him, others deem it utterly outrageous to slap a child. It is at this point that Breithaupt's considerations of empathy come in. After all, the reader is indeed inclined to take sides with either one position or the other, even though, in contrast to Breithaupt's rather static model, I would suggest that, especially in a multiperspectival text such as *The Slap*, this need not result in a permanent decision but can and often does change continuously throughout the narrative. Similarly, situational empathy may come in, based on whether one as a reader has already experienced a similar situation in real life.

Despite the unstable and potentially changing degree or stability of empathy, then, textual features, such as the shifting focalization of the novel, are deliberate strategies in Tsiolkas's novel to elicit the readers' empathy. It is, for instance, noteworthy that the slapping described in the novel's first chapter is focalized through Hector, Harry's cousin, who defends his relative's behavior. In this context, Jessica Gildersleeve has aptly remarked that "the focalisation of the event through Hector [...] actively positions the reader with his family, rather than Hugo's" (Gildersleeve 88), the family of the victim. This does not mean that the reader automatically feels empathy with Hector and Harry's position. Yet, by including only the inner thoughts of Hector, the text creates a particular bond between reader and focalizer that may hence facilitate empathy with Hector's reaction. In this regard, passages both before and after the slapping are of interest. Initially, Hector notes how Hugo apparently puts another boy, namely Harry's son, at risk: "Hector froze. He's going to hit him. He's going to belt Rocco with that bat" (Tsiolkas 40). After the slap, the text, then, observes that Hector "was glad that the boy had been punished" (Tsiolkas 41). By suggesting that the slap was only a means to protect another child, Hector's focalization hence justifies the slapping and invites readers to feel about the incident like Hector.

Importantly, however, as I have observed above, the characters toward whom one feels empathic may change during the course of the narrative. In contrast to the description of Hugo as a spoilt and misbehaving child through Hector's eyes, the chapter focalized through Rosie, Hugo's mother, shows how her bodily attachment to her son is a way to overcome her postnatal depression. By "los[ing] herself in him," she can "set herself free" (Tsiolkas 239) from the inability to "feel love for the child [she] had brought into the world" (Tsiolkas 238) that she experienced shortly after the birth of her son. This change of perspective may provoke sympathy for her and her position and switch a reader's assessment of the incident itself. Moreover, readers with similar experiences may even feel empathy with her. The different and shifting focalizing instances offer emotional insights into the characters that would not be possible in non-multiperspectival heterodiegetic narratives with internal focalization. Focalization may therefore trigger different, shifting, and potentially seemingly mutually exclusive empathic alliances and responses.

However, even though empathic alliances may change throughout the narrative, at the end of the novel *The Slap* strengthens the affiliation between readers and the character of Richie especially strongly. Again, it does so through the description of a conflict, though a far less central one than the eponymous slap. At one point in the narrative, Connie, who is a friend of Richie's and has an affair with Hector, tells Richie that Hector "raped" her (Tsiolkas 181). In contrast to Richie, the reader soon finds out that she is lying in a passage describing the apparent assault that is focalized through her. In the final chapter, Richie meets Hector at the swimming pool, subsequently breaks down emotionally, and tells close friends about the rape. Soon, all of them inform Aisha, Hector's wife, about the alleged molestation in the presence of Connie. In contrast to Richie's hopes that Connie would clarify the situation, she not only accuses her best friend of lying but additionally outs him: "'It's not true.' [...] 'I promise it's not true.' [...] 'He's obsessed with Hector,' she spluttered. 'He's fucking sick. He's making it all up[.']" (Tsiolkas 465). At this point, the text invites sympathy, because readers feel for Richie, even if they cannot adopt his point of view because of the epistemic distance. This side-taking is the result of the knowledge discrepancy between readers and the storyworld, in turn a direct consequence of the narrative's multiperspectival structure. In contrast to Richie, the reader has known all along that Connie's allegations have been false and therefore sympathizes with him, since s/he knows that Richie only wanted to help his friend. At the same time, readers may not only feel for Richie, but may also feel *with* him. When, after Connie's revelation, "[h]e didn't call out, he did not cry" (Tsiolkas 465), readers may feel his disillusionment, again because they are aware that Richie believed his friend and only wanted to assist her. The scene of his outing as well as Connie's wrong accusations of Richie hence create an empathic resonance. As readers, we are made to feel with Richie, because we know of his good intentions and the fact that he has been treated unfairly. What the text does here is to evoke *"broadcast strategic empathy"* (Keen, *Novel* 142). Regardless of readers' sexualities, they are invited to feel empathy with Richie because presumably everyone knows about the experience of being treated unfairly. This broadcast strategic empathy, I would like to argue, is a deliberate strategy of Tsiolkas to raise greater understanding for marginal sexualities. In this sense, through the fact that the chapter focalized through Richie comes last and the accusations about the alleged rape are never cleared up, *The Slap* invites greater understanding for those whose subjectivities are marginalized within society.

Trauma and Empathic Unsettlement in Gail Jones's *Five Bells* (2011)

Gail Jones's *Five Bells* is an entirely different text from *The Slap*. The narrative is set in Sydney on a particular Saturday and follows its four character-focalizers on their individual, vastly different ways through the city. James and Ellie, two friends from childhood, meet years again after their romance as teenagers; the Chinese-Australian woman Pei Xing visits her former prison guard during the Cultural Revolution, who now also lives in Sydney; and the Irishwoman Catherine reminisces about her dead brother Brendan. In contrast to the generally realistic frame of Tsiolkas's novel, Jones's more modernist technique allows the stories of the different narrative strands to bounce off each other even though the characters never meet knowingly. As a consequence of the latter, *Five Bells*, in contrast to *The Slap*, is not exacerbating conflict between characters.

This, as I have suggested previously, also has an effect on how narrative empathy operates in the novel in that the text does not privilege one focalizing perspective over the others in the same way as Tsiolkas's narrative. Still, Jones's novel is likely to generate strong empathic responses among readers. Studying how narrative empathy features in the novel, I want to argue, can therefore add productively to existing discussions of the novel. In order to do so it is helpful to approach the text from a trauma studies perspective.

Robert Dixon has convincingly argued for the significance of trauma in the novel (7–12). Indeed, most of the character-focalizers experience some kind of trauma: for James it is the drowning of a schoolchild he was supposed to supervise, for Catherine it is her brother's death and for Pei Xing it is the experience of detainment during the Cultural Revolution (Jones 53, 105, 155). The significance of trauma for the novel also opens up the capacity for narrative empathy, since, as Dominick LaCapra (37–38) has pointed out, both are tightly intertwined. He has noted the important role of empathy to deal with trauma (LaCapra 78), though he similarly cautions that this must not lead to "the total fusion of self and other" (LaCapra 38). He offers a way out of this impasse with his concept of empathic unsettlement, which is "a kind of virtual experience through which one puts oneself in the other's position while recognizing the difference of that position and hence not taking the other's place" (LaCapra 78). The proximity between trauma and empathy also becomes evident, when Keen argues that *"empathetic responses to fictional characters and situations occur more readily for negative feeling states, whether or not a match in details of experience exists*" (*Novel* 72). She gives as examples "negative affective states, such as those provoked by undergoing persecution, suffering, grieving, and experiencing painful obstacles" (Keen, *Novel* 71). Against this background, the protagonist for whom the interrelation between trauma and empathy is most salient and on whom I therefore want to focus subsequently is Pei Xing.

In this context, Dixon has noted that "[b]y including Pei Xing's story of the Cultural Revolution in *Five Bells*, Jones is therefore extending the now classic American and European cases to recognize traumatic events in Asia and, at the same time, their proximity to Australia as a European settler nation located in Asia" (9). Extending this argument in light of LaCapra's considerations discussed above, I suggest that Pei Xing's narrative is significant not only because it challenges the dominance of Western-centric notions of trauma, but also because it enables empathic unsettlement. This is not to say that it cancels Western experiences of trauma. Rather, it extends the view on trauma by including other, less known traumatic experiences. It does so when the text describes the misery of her imprisonment focalized through her: "At first there was only retching despair and a nightmare of foreboding. Pei Xing waited to die. She was cold and cramped and could not imagine a future. She was filled with a grief of monstrous inexactitude. Day and night she heard sobbing, and random brutal shouts" (Jones 155). Here, her suffering becomes tangible, which, keeping in mind Keen's finding about the particular capacity of negative sensations to create empathy, facilitates empathic responses. Yet, importantly, since this narrative is located in a Chinese, rather than Australian, context, it refutes "the total fusion of self and other" that LaCapra (38) criticizes and instead allows for empathic unsettlement. After all, the novel's implied reader, who, I would argue, is Australian or Anglo-Saxon rather than Chinese, can feel with Pei Xing, even though s/he is well aware that her/his own position differs markedly from Pei Xing's position as a victim of the Chinese Cultural Revolution.

Of course, readers may also feel with other characters. When, for example, James writes a short, formal condolence letter to the parents of the deceased child, the text subsequently foregrounds his actual emotions that he could not express in writing: "James had wanted to say: *Forgive me, forgive me, something went wrong. The world collapsed and Amy was under it. There is no word I can offer, there is nothing I can say, that will make things right*" (Jones 199). Here, through James's focalization, one literally feels his grief and readers may well empathize with him, even if they have not been in a similar situation themselves. Significantly, then, it is not that the form of empathy that readers express with Pei Xing differs from the one with James. Neither do I want to suggest that there are any textual features that make it more likely for readers to feel with Pei Xing rather than James or any other of the characters. In this sense, *Five Bells* differs from *The Slap* in that the empathy that the text triggers with Pei Xing is not a result of the narrative's multiperspectivity. Instead, the empathy with Pei Xing fulfils a different *function* than the empathic responses for other characters precisely because of its potential for empathic unsettlement.

In order to consider why this is so, I would like to point to existing scholarly discussions of the novel. Literary critics have conventionally read *Five Bells* in the context of multiculturalism and transnationalism (Dixon 1; Kossew 279; Kušnír 469; Midalia 46). The empathy with Pei Xing, I propose, has to be read in this very context, since it helps create the vision of a multicultural Australia and transnational world. After all, the empathy with Pei Xing highlights that what "we and the other have in common lies in the realm of physical and emotional pain" (Koopman 242) and hence transcends national, cultural and historical boundaries. What *Five Bells* evokes here is *"broadcast strategic empathy"* (Keen, *Novel* 142). Through empathy with Pei Xing, rather than Ellie, James or Catherine, *Five Bells*, then, emphasizes that what binds humans together exceeds notions such as nation or ethnicity. In this sense, the empathy with Pei Xing, like the one with Richie in *The Slap*, promotes diversity and calls for an appreciation of marginalized groups, in the case of Jones's narrative migrants.

Conclusion

In this essay, I have been interested in the question of how narrative empathy operates in contemporary Australian multiperspectival novels. My main argument has been that the multiperspectivity of a narrative generates empathy particularly if the text foregrounds conflict between focalizers. To this end, I have focused on two different texts, a multiperspectival novel that exacerbates conflict between characters, Christos Tsiolkas's *The Slap*, and one that does not do so, Gail Jones's *Five Bells*. As I have shown in my textual readings, the multiperspectival structure of *The Slap* triggers empathic responses with the resulting effect of privileging some perspectives over others. By showing particularly prominent moments of the narrative through the eyes of merely one focalizer, for instance the slap through Hector or Connie's deceitfulness through Richie, and voicing the inner thoughts of this character only, the narrative creates a special bond between readers and character-focalizers. This invites the first to empathize with these characters' positions more readily than with others. The readers' responses therefore function as a means to foreground these perspectives at the expense of others. In *Five Bells*, this is not the case, since the narrative does not highlight conflict between the characters to the same degree as Tsiolkas's novel. This does not imply a lack of readerly empathy, however. There is, then, no simple relationship between multiperspectivity and narrative empathy in that different texts make use of it differently.

Yet, while Tsiolkas and Jones's novels differ in the ways in which narrative empathy features, its function, I have suggested, is similar in both texts. After all, the empathy with both Richie and Pei Xing serves to advocate a greater understanding for marginalized groups and an embracement of a diverse society. Importantly, like Keen (*Novel* 22), I remain wary of the capacity of readerly empathy to translate into better actions in the real world. Yet, I do believe that narrative empathy has an "ethical potential" (Koopman 241) in both *The Slap* and *Five Bells*. It is exactly because of this that studying narrative empathy in Australian literature can fruitfully contribute to and enrich existing literary debates.

Notes

1 I would like to thank Jean-François Vernay, Dennis Haskell, Sarah Heinz, and the two anonymous reviewers for their helpful suggestions.
2 This distinction is, however, not always made and Mandy Treagus, for instance, mistakenly argues that *The Slap* includes "multiple narrators from different perspectives" (5), a view that Glyn Davis (175) also seems to hold. For a discussion of the difference between narration and focalization in the context of *The Slap*, see Bonnici (122).
3 Until the early twentieth century, the term "sympathy" also covered the contemporary meaning of empathy (Keen, *Novel* 4).
4 All quotes by Keen (*Novel*) in italics also appear in italics in the original.

Works Cited

Batson, C. Daniel, and Nadia Y. Ahmad. "Using Empathy to Improve Intergroup Attitudes and Relations." *Social Issues and Policy Review*, vol. 3, no. 1, 2009, pp. 141–177. *SPSSI*, doi: 10.1111/j.1751-2409.2009.01013.x.

Bonnici, Thomas. "Multicultural Australia in Fiction." *Acta Scientiarum: Language and Culture*, vol. 34, no. 1, 2012, pp. 121–123. *DOAJ*, doi: 10. 4025/actascilangcult.v34i1.12766.

Breithaupt, Fritz. *Kulturen der Empathie.* Suhrkamp, 2009.

Davis, Glyn. "*The Slap*'s Resonances: Multiculturalism and Adolescence in Tsiolkas' Australia." *Interactions: Studies in Communication & Culture*, vol. 3, no. 2, 2012, pp. 173–186. *EBSCOhost*, doi: 10.1386/iscc.3.2.173_1.

Dixon, Robert. "Invitation to the Voyage: Reading Gail Jones's *Five Bells*." *Journal of the Association for the Study of Australian Literature*, vol. 12, no. 3, 2012, pp. 1–17. *openjournals*, openjournals.library.sydney.edu.au/index.php/JASAL/article/view/9827/9715.

Dunlop, Nicholas. "Suburban Space and Multicultural Identities in Christos Tsiolkas's *The Slap*." *Antipodes*, vol. 30, no. 1, 2016, pp. 5–16. *JSTOR*, www.jstor.org/stable/10.13110/antipodes.30.1.0005.

Gildersleeve, Jessica. *Christos Tsiolkas: The Utopian Vision.* Cambria P, 2017.

Hartner, Marcus. "Multiperspectivity." *Handbook of Narratology: Volume 1*, edited by Peter Hühn et al. De Gruyter, 2014, pp. 353–363.

Herman, David. "Cognitive Narratology." *Handbook of Narratology*, edited by Peter Hühn et al. De Gruyter, 2009, pp. 30–43. *DeGruyter eBooks*, doi: 10.1515/9783110217445.30.

Hogan, Patrick Colm. "The Epilogue of Suffering: Heroism, Empathy, Ethics." *SubStance*, vol. 30, no. 1/2, 2001. *JSTOR*, www.jstor.org/stable/3685508.

Jones, Gail. *Five Bells.* Vintage, 2012.

Keen, Suzanne. *Empathy and the Novel.* Oxford UP, 2007.

Keen, Suzanne. "Empathy Studies." *A Companion to Literary Theory*, edited by David H. Richter. John Wiley & Sons, 2018, pp. 126–138. *Wiley Online Library*, doi: 10.1002/9781118958933.ch10.

Keen, Suzanne. "Narrative Empathy." *Handbook of Narratology: Volume 2*, edited by Peter Hühn et al. De Gruyter, 2014, pp. 521–530.

Koopman, Emy. "Reading the Suffering of Others: The Ethical Possibilities of ›Empathic Unsettlement‹." *Journal of Literary Theory*, vol. 4, no. 2, 2010, pp. 235–252. *De Gruyter Online Journals*, doi: 10.1515/JLT.2010.015.

Kossew, Sue. "City of Words: Haunting Legacies in Gail Jones's *Five Bells*." *Re-Inventing the Postcolonial (in the) Metropolis*, edited by Cecile Sandten and Annika Bauer. Brill, 2016, pp. 277–289. *Brill*, doi: 10.1163/9789004328761_018.

Kušnír, Jaroslav. "Diasporic 'Home' and Transnational Identities in Gail Jones's *Five Bells*." *Diasporic Constructions of Home and Belonging*, edited by Florian Kläger and Klaus Stierstorfer. De Gruyter, 2015, pp. 465–477. *EBSCOhost*, web.b.ebscohost.com.uaccess.univie.ac.at/ehost/ebookviewer/ebook/bmxlYmtfXzEyNTA3MDZfX0FO0?sid=b6b4fc1c75b04705973ff5c-c685a1571@sessionmgr104&vid=0&format=EB&rid=1.

LaCapra, Dominick. *Writing History, Writing Trauma.* Johns Hopkins UP, 2014.

McCann, Andrew. *Christos Tsiolkas and the Fiction of Critique: Politics, Obscenity, Celebrity.* Anthem P, 2015. *JSTOR*, www.jstor.org/stable/j.ctt1gxp724.

Midalia, Susan. "The Idea of Place: Reading for Pleasure and the Workings of Power." *English in Australia*, vol. 47, no. 3, 2012, pp. 44–51. *Informit Humanities & Social Sciences Collection*, searchinformitcomau.ezproxy1.library.usyd.edu.au/documentSummary;dn=100862829435512;res=IELHSS.

Neumann, Birgit, and Ansgar Nünning. *An Introduction to the Study of Narrative Fiction*. Klett, 2011.

Peer, W. van, and H. Pander Maat. "Perspectivation and Sympathy: Effects of Narrative Point of View." *Empirical Approaches to Literature and Aesthetics*, edited by Roger J. Kreuz and Mary Sue MacNealy. Ablex, 1996, pp. 143–154.

Serino, A. et al. "I Feel What You Feel if You Are Similar to Me." *PLoS ONE*, vol. 4, no. 3, 2009, e4930. *PLOS ONE*, doi: 10.1371/journal.pone.0004930.

Sommer, Roy. "Other Stories, Other Minds: The Intercultural Potential of Cognitive Approaches to Narrative." *Stories and Minds: Cognitive Approaches to Literary Narrative*, edited by Lars Bernaerts et al. U of Nebraska P, 2013, pp. 155–174.

Treagus, Mandy. "Queering the Mainstream: *The Slap* and 'Middle' Australia." *Journal of the Association for the Study of Australian Literature*, vol. 12, no. 3, 2012, pp. 1–9. *openjournals*, openjournals.library.sydney.edu.au/index.php/JASAL/article/view/9831.

Tsiolkas, Christos. *The Slap*. Atlantic Books, 2010.

Vernay, Jean-François. "Bridging the Two Cultures: Literary Studies Through the Looking Glass of Cognitive Science." *Lingua. Language and Culture*, vol. 18, no. 2, 2019, pp. 111–127. *Central and Eastern European Online Library*, www.ceeol.com/search/article-detail?id=827714.

Zunshine, Lisa. "Introduction to Cognitive Literary Studies." *The Oxford Handbook of Cognitive Literary Studies*, edited by Lisa Zunshine. Oxford UP, 2015, pp. 1–9.

3   Contemplating Affects: The Mystery of Emotion in Charlotte Wood's *The Weekend*

Victoria Reeve

Introduction

Jude had no illusions. (Wood 2019, 1)

Charlotte Wood's novel, *The Weekend,* tells the story of three friends, Jude, Wendy, and Adele, who have gone to the holiday house of their friend, Sylvie, 11 months after her death to clear the place ahead of sale. The novel opens on Jude's consciousness, which includes this focalized statement of her having no illusions. Describing Jude's thoughts about her thoughts, the statement marks an instance of recursive thinking (see Tomasello 16), whereby Jude takes a stance toward herself that, although mediated by the narrative voice and the use of third person, nonetheless performs shifts in perspective indicative of oscillations between constructions of subjective and objective appraisals of self.

Jude, apparently, has no illusions about cognitive decline and death (the friends are in their 70s). And yet, now that I have read the novel and moved beyond the limits of its opening paragraphs, I find myself inferring something else – something related to this but beyond those feelings that Jude openly expresses. I call this sense of something else *the mystery of emotion* because I refer to interpretations involved in reading that go beyond the comprehension of characters like Jude or the story as a whole to include effects on personal experience called upon through imagining the story (see Feldman Barrett xiii; Armstrong 113). Like Jude, I involve myself in shifting perspectives that include construing an objective stance toward my own experience. With myself as the reader in this instance, oscillating between the text and my experiences through the identification of partial correspondences, the mystery arises as to why and how I have become involved in reading. Although my reading depends upon the common ground of language and culture (Tomasello 20, 59) that I share with the novel's author (implied or otherwise), in representing that common ground to me in novel ways, *The Weekend* has led me to reappraise and reinterpret aspects of my experience.

In this chapter I argue that the mystery of emotion, as a question of involvement, derives from emotion as a form of reasoning, brought within the parameters of thought as an affectual process. It is through the intimacies of experience as something that recursively moves through bodily apprehensions, interpretive (affective) expressions, and the comprehension of such in cultural contexts, that emotion becomes the recognizable outcome of a given experience.

On Being Affected by Reading

I feel affected by the statement, "Jude had no illusions." I take Jude's lack of illusions to represent a particular emotion – anger – though, in the novel, it takes the form of suffocated rage which Jude redirects as annoyance and frustration. I was affected by the statement because I recalled my mother saying something very similar, repeatedly, during my childhood. My mother, who struggled with her mental wellbeing throughout her life, spoke her rage out loud on a daily basis around the home, sometimes involving long hours of brooding hushed conversations with herself and extended rants. She would often burst into the room where my twin sister and I were playing to perform her rage with wild eyes that did not seem to see us. As a child, I had access to her thoughts in ways that few people experience outside literature. I grew up in someone else's mind – listening to the litany of offenses others had committed, hearing the details of such through the distorting echoes of grief and rage that characterized her self-expression. So it was that, in some measure, I recalled this when I read that "Jude had no illusions." I did not recall the details immediately, but later recognized them in the affective "huh!" that I experienced on reading that statement for the first time.

Paul B. Armstrong argues that "The comprehension of a story requires active participation by the recipient, who must project relations between the parts that are told and their probable configuration in the whole that seems to be forming" (Armstrong 116). It is an oscillating, to-and-fro process whereby readers come to identify with aspects of the narrative – sometimes with specific characters. John Frow describes identification with "character as an effect of desire, understood not as "someone's" desire but as a structure forming the imaginary unity of subjects in their relation to the imaginary unity of objects." Identification thus involves the reader in the formation of character through the recognition of aspects of self. Literary character might be understood to be, in this sense at least, "an effect of the 'self-recognition' of a subject in its dispersal through the multiple positions offered to it by a text" (Frow 2016, 53–54).

Jude's having no illusions thus became recognizable to me in partial terms. I reformed these correspondences in a reappraisal of personal experience that resulted in my identifying the statement as the summary of insults and frustrations my mother had experienced. This I translated back to Jude, who, unlike my mother, swallows her rage. Understanding that Wood was inviting comparisons in setting out the lives of these three women, each facing old age on her own terms, each without the financial or social life raft that a husband might offer in a world of gender inequality (see Wood 51), I found further relevancies. I saw how Wendy's academic life and self-expression was unlike that otherwise conventionally permitted a woman (particularly of her generation [see 110]), and how her achievements afforded her no alibi for her resentful children (16, 55, 94, 114, 116, 117, 119, 165, 222–223) who might have forgiven her, perhaps, had she been a father rather than a mother.

Wendy, of the three friends, is financially secure. She has meaningful work as an academic and is in a very different position to Jude and Adele. She is nonetheless still caught in a social world where gender determines status and delimits a person's role as much as value. The inequalities of that dynamic are especially marked in Wendy's difficult relationship with her children; but her situation overall stands in contrast to the positions of Jude, a retired restaurant manager, "glorified waitress" (78), hostess, or maître-d (it is not clear which), and Adele, an unemployed actor – both childless. These two women, as it turns out, have no safety net, and no life raft with which to navigate the choppy waters of old age and looming indigence. Adele enters the narrative in a state of financial crisis and needing to borrow money from Wendy; but Jude's fall is the central point here because the turnaround is so surprising yet retrospectively evident, causing the reader to reappraise Jude's situation from the outset. As my reading of "Jude had no illusions" will show, this reappraisal brings greater depth of meaning to that statement.

Jude is the kept lover of a wealthy married man, Daniel Schwartz – their relationship spanning 40 years (78). It is Jude's sudden realization of what she has been deferring and suppressing for these last decades that contradicts her having no illusions. She has been living an illusion in fact. Her perpetual state of suppressed rage throughout the weekend she spends with her friends is there for a reason. But it is not organized in ways that make the meaning of her feelings immediately apparent to Jude herself. Rather, it is the reader who must make this interpretation.

Jude is left stunned and bereft when she discovers that, not only has her lover suffered a catastrophic stroke, but her situation in life has drastically altered. When confronted with a text revealing that Daniel will be forever unavailable to her, it becomes clear that his affairs have now fallen into hostile hands (that of his wife and adult children). Jude can only utter ("in disbelief"), "I don't know what this means" (250). She has deferred all comprehension of the precarity of her situation, transferring her annoyance and frustration onto other scenarios and individuals: for much of the novel she is aggravated all round, by her friends, and just about anything she lays her eyes upon – anything and everyone, that is, except Daniel. Thus, by the time I reached the close of the narrative, "Jude had no illusions" seemed the kind of statement made by someone who, being used to her frustrations, reluctantly accepts an insurmountable wrong. What is wrong – what is made apparent by the reappraisal of Jude's position by these surprising events at the end – comes down to those inequalities that leave women like Jude and Adele vulnerable and dependent on others rather than self-sufficient.

The reversal of Jude's situation – from a woman seemingly without financial cares, to a woman in dire circumstances – caused me to look more closely at her underlying aggression. With deeper reflection, I saw abnegation encoded in the statement's assertion, and I realized that Jude's anger with her friends was exacerbated by her inability to direct anger toward Daniel. Daniel visits Jude weekly *or* monthly (156), indicating that there are constraints upon her interaction with him: "Jude's life depended on an opaque acceptance of many facets of Daniel's life" (33). Indeed, implicated in the vagrancy of his presence in her life is the possibility that his distance might on occasion be wielded as a form of reproach at Jude behaving unpleasantly by getting annoyed about other people – her friends, in particular (7, 9, 84, 207). Given her financial dependence on him, Jude's anger about the unequal nature of their relationship could not be safely expressed. Thus, Jude, "asking for nothing, expecting nothing, from Daniel" (220), defines "her code: you did not refuse what was offered" (7). This then accounts for Wendy's observation that "Every time you went to

[Jude's] place it looked somehow different. Daniel's money was a steady, generous tide, washing up new things, taking old ones away" (42). Daniel's generosity, in other words, is to give *and* take – meaning that his lover is kept on her toes, unable to set down roots in the form of attachment to things. There is no room for eccentricity to develop in Jude except in her attachment to him. With his generosity, and the secretive nature of their relationship (42, 70, 97, 98), and just these few friends – Sylvie (now deceased), Wendy, and Adele – Jude is left otherwise isolated, hidden away, and possibly even alienated from the wider world (see, for example, 123).

That "Her life was as clean and bare as a bone" now seems tragic – something that was not apparent when I viewed it as an esthetic choice. But, with "The rooms of her apartment [...] uncluttered by the past" such that "Nobody would have to plough through dusty boxes and cupboards full of rubbish for Jude" when she died (5), this esthetic now stands out as indicative of a woman constrained and controlled. If my comprehension of Jude's vulnerability was deferred by the brusqueness of her confidence and her self-serving acts of generosity (see 7) – with that generosity perhaps necessitated by the constant renewal of objects in the apartment (before Jude has a chance to leave her mark upon them) – it was awakened by Adele's focalized statement that "What happened was what was always going to happen to Jude" (251). My reappraisal was crystallized by Jude's acknowledgment that "her apartment [...] was probably no longer her apartment" (255). Indeed, it never was. The neutrality of the furnishings suggests as much. Daniel, it would seem (despite never discussing the matter with Jude [3]), though he may not have actively thought about what would happen if Jude were to die one day, was (by the constant flow of his generosity) sub-consciously making preparations to erase her completely. Jude, still in shock, is brought to the threshold of this realization, when she tries and fails to see Daniel in hospital. With Daniel's wife Helena and his two children who, "Without looking in the women's direction [...] walked with their arms linked past the waiting room" (252), cementing Daniel's denial of her existence.

The Interpretive Capacities of Emotion as an Organizing Concept

Armstrong defines emotions as "mixed products of biology and culture that are better thought of as variable, internally heterogenous populations than logical categories or universal classes with fixed neurobiological foundations" (21). On this view, "language and narrative are biocultural hybrids," each a "product of variable but constrained interactions between brain, body, and world and not universals that are homologous to logical structures of the mind" (24). Variably constituted in neuronal and cultural terms, yet somehow recognizable, Armstrong's approach to emotion makes it sound very much like genre. Indeed, Lisa Feldman Barrett gives an account of the brain as fundamentally involved in categorizing and she outlines processes of meaning making consistent with genre theory (see, for example, Frow 10; Feldman Barrett 35). Emotions as categories have a specific focus, organizing such relations in terms of culturally recognizable feeling states and their associated actions, affects, and effects. I want to avoid tracking specific literary genres and emotion (see Carroll 125; Storey 101–178), however, and rely instead on genre as an organizing strategy in the making of meaning – one that groups larger concepts by linking parts within a whole to other parts within otherwise different wholes in ways that are consistent with Armstrong's approach to meaning. For Armstrong, interpretation, involving the reading of signs, finds its "neurobiological basis" in "the reactivations of simulation" in terms that are "partial and [which] can be configured in different ways" (120). Thus, figurative patterns or gestalts supply a model for cognition (see 17), whereby "gaps and indeterminacies," which are "a familiar feature of perceptual experience" (139), are resolved by the reader of narrative "by the intertwining of different modalities" – different gestalts or patterns of experience (133) – creating "an illusion of presence and facilitate[ing] immersion in a fictional world" (138).

Emotion, following Armstrong and Feldman Barrett, is a semantic category, rather than something that happens in a specific region of the brain. It is an interpretive stance taken toward bodily feelings and thoughts, within a given context (Feldman Barrett 42–55). Forming a semiotic system based on embodied experiences, emotions are the first stage in processes of expression and communication through, what Michael Tomasello calls, protoconversations (54–55). Shaped by cultural values, emotions are the means by which we select and organize a range of internal feelings and sensations into states of being within a range of contexts.

It was through the organizing effects of reading and emotion – whereby identification enabled the recognition of parts of experience across two distinct wholes (the fictional Jude and my memory of my mother) – that I was affected in my reading of *The Weekend*. My reappraisal of Jude, drawing on my personal experiences, involved reappraisals in personal terms as well. I already understood that much of what I had found distressing in my mother's behavior (and which was obviously distressing for her) was caused, or at least exacerbated, by similar frustrations, organized around gender inequality. These frustrations centered on gendered barriers to meaningful work in the 1960s and 1970s, my mother's inability (as an unmarried woman) to secure a housing loan when cheap housing became available, and other tragic denials of her social status as an equal member of society (predominantly clustered around her experience of having been raped by a soldier when a member of the Australian Women's Army during World War Two, and her inability to have this acknowledged and compensated by the Department of Veteran Affairs). Though, of course, there were other factors to my mother's distress, the intensity of her suffering, and the suffering experienced by her children, owed a lot to gender inequality. Her angry and sometimes brutal reaction to her frustrating situation, together with the poverty she experienced as a single parent (homelessness loomed throughout my infancy and my brother suffered malnutrition), had a huge impact on us all.

In comprehending Jude, the compassion that I had already organized around the realization that my mother's anger at society had been redirected and expressed within the home, was prompted, renewed, and reformed by the compassion that I felt for Jude. Of course, *The Weekend* is not in any way an equal comparison to my recollected experiences. Jude's ranting (if it can be called that) takes place in her thoughts. But because my mother's speech incorporated other perspectives, it seemed to bear some correspondence to the effects created in Wood's text. This may be an effect of my unique experiences as a child, hearing what I came to regard as internal speech spoken out loud, combined with my understanding of narrative poetics. Suffice to say, part of what affected me was the correspondence that I found between the narrative voice of *The Weekend* and my mother's unusual self-expression.

Importantly, I was affected by my thoughts – by my understanding of Wood's text, and the correlations I found there. And this is significant – if stating the obvious – because cognition stands at the seeming extremity of recursive processes of interpretation, which we might say begin, in a sense, with interoception. If feeling forms in response to interoception (Damasio 24–25; Feldman Barrett 56), and affect is the expression of feeling in bodily processes, then emotion, as the interpretation of bodily experience in environmental and social contexts (Feldman Barrett 72, 32–41; see Solomon 11), is a form of reasoning – one that stands upon the bodily apprehensions of feeling and affect (see Zajonc 31; Forgas 387–390) while being part of that affective chain. Thoughts, in other words, are contemplating affects.

Although a number of philosophers have touched upon the role of thought in respect to emotion (Solomon 4, 5, 7, 10), thought's affectual status is often overlooked, with the focus on its semantic content drawing attention from this; yet meaning affects us, and this is the function of thought as affect: it organizes experience in ways that are, in turn, affecting.

Grammatical Mood and Perspective-Taking

Bearing resemblances to focalized perspective and even free indirect discourse (see Miller 42), my mother's speech became aligned with both the narrative voice and character perspective. This alignment perhaps accounts for another aspect of my reading of Jude. Because I had come to understand my mother's anger as, in some sense, part and parcel of a desperate attempt to counter deeper feelings of self-loathing, I read self-contempt in the statement, "Jude had no illusions." Although I am importing assumptions formed by my reading of my mother's speech, in light of my reappraisal of Jude, I find a hint of awareness in the ironic distance that lies between the narrative voice and this focalized statement. This awareness slides between narratorial and characterological constructions. It is messy, in some respects, but the distinctions of multiple perspectives – Jude as herself, Jude as the perceiver of herself, the narrative voice articulating an "objective" perspective of Jude as she sees herself, and the implied reader, taking all this in – can be found in Wood's text.

Perspective-taking is an important element in the social construction of emotion (Tomasello 16–17). It is embedded in language and emphasized in styles of speech deployed in literary works (see Genette 1983, 73). Wood demonstrates an awareness of this early in the novel through an instance of perspective-taking within Jude's thoughts. Lying in bed, worried about aging and cognitive decline, not having any illusions, Jude "pictured the soft grey sphere of her brain and remembered lambs' brains on a plate. She used to enjoy eating brains," we are told; "it was one of the dishes she ordered often with Daniel" (2):

> But at first bite the thing yielded in her mouth, too rich, like just-soft butter; tepid and pale grey, the colour and taste of moths or death. In that moment she was shocked into a vision of the three lambs, each one its own conscious self, with its own senses, its intimate pleasures and pains. After a mouthful she could not go on, and Daniel ate the rest. She had wanted to say, "I don't want to die." Of course she did not say that. Instead, she asked Daniel about the novel he was reading. (2)

Jude's earlier enjoyment of lambs' brains is called into question by her sudden revulsion for them when seeing them as "three bald, poached splodges on a bed of green" (2). Unadorned of the usual breadcrumbs, Jude is repulsed; but "She ate them, of course" (2). Her affective response interrupts her intention, however, and she gives up on the meal. Her thoughts, having become involved in the process of eating, have further affected her. Thinking of the lambs themselves, as whole beings whose body parts (the brains) are now before her, Jude focuses her attention on the brain's role in sensation and feeling and from there arrives at the idea of lambs as creatures of consciousness. Wood, in this way, demonstrates how our thoughts complicate our affective states to add layers of diversity in terms of valence and intensity (see Feldman Barrett 72) through perspective-taking.

Narrative mood, as the grammatical instantiation of perspective, supplies the means by which the literary work establishes nested intimacies like that demonstrated by Jude. We might say that Jude is performing the narrative voice in embodied terms by taking the lamb's brain into her mouth. The passage thus functions as an allegory of narrative speech in ways that emphasize the strange intimacy of speaking as another. Distinctions of grammatical mood are relevant to Gérard Genette's notion of focalization and to free indirect discourse (see 1983, 73; 1980, 161–162): when mood goes awry (that is, when tenses seem at cross purposes by not corresponding to the position of the speaker), it means that the narrative voice (as a grammatically instituted point of view) is inflected with the spatiotemporal markers (in the form of grammatical tense) indicative of another point of view (that of character). Basically, the tenses in a given statement do not match the grammatical parameters for the speaker of that statement, yet the anomaly makes sense as the insertion of another consciousness or subjectivity – another point of view.

This splitting of states of being involves complexities of feeling, in that the narrative voice, inflected with another subjectivity, will, through its word choices, convey something of the narrating subjectivity's attitude or feeling toward what it describes (whether this feeling is pleasant or unpleasant, for example). Though the narrative voice may not articulate feeling or opinion as plainly as Jude's experience has it (whereby she stands in relation to the lamb's brain as the narrative voice stands in relation to character), some relation between the spoken narrative and its content is nonetheless evident in its coherence as speech, simply because we understand speakers to be invested in the subject matter of which they speak.

Whether interest or disinterest, engagement or disgust are openly performed in the narrative voice, emotion as a linguistic pattern embedded in speech, is, at the very least, established in the deontological markers that are implicated in all narratorial speech. As my analysis of my reading reveals, the nested intimacies of perspective-taking evident in narrative are further complicated by the to-and-fro mediation of correspondences identified through reading. Comprehension thus involves emotion in those processes of reasoning that result in identification.

If emotions, as constructs, are the effects of organizing experiences in the intentionally collective ways of culture, then recursive thought (thinking about feeling, context, affect, emotion, etc.) introduces those meaning values in ways that sometimes intensify and diversify our personal and shared experiences in the collaborative processes of social construction (see Tomasello 90). It is this intensification and diversification that we most likely identify as internally experienced emotion. I can unpack this process on my own terms in Wood's characterization of Jude having no illusions and not wanting to die: the leap from disgust (over what she is eating) to fear (of death) makes perfect sense once we untangle the layers of cultural belief and personal experience that contribute to it. If Jude is aware of the meanings that underlie the superficial value of Daniel's generosity, she must surely realize that she has become a problem in old age. Too old to be a mistress (51), she seems to intuit the consequences of Daniel's erasure of her presence through the constant flow of the things he gives her, resulting in the bare-boned existence that is her life. Her death would be convenient for him, and her plaintive thought, "I don't want to die," seems to accept the strength of his wishes, as though she has read his mind, just as I have read hers. "I don't want to die," she thinks, seemingly out of the blue – as though she has no say in it; as though Daniel merely wishing it so, would make it so. Framed within her thoughts on cognitive decline and her not having any illusions, the connection between her perceived redundancy and death makes sense to me. At some point, she must bow out gracefully, and die – that is what she realizes, on some level, as she gives up on the lambs' brains. She has already prepared the way by absolving Daniel of any need to tidy up the mess of her life: her (always) newly furnished apartment would, upon her death, quickly resume a tidy impersonal status within his property portfolio.

This is the semantic outcome of the affective charge that stirred in me when I connected these episodes. These meanings are not there for Jude to disentangle, though I use language that involves her in my thought processes. Jude, of course, functions within a sign system that provokes the simulation of her experience in my imagination, and I read those simulations on these terms. But even if we extend to Jude the possibility of existence, she must remain at the threshold of such realizations for the surprising reappraisal of her character to take place. Her thoughts must remain obliquely configured; her anger suppressed so that it might be redirected as annoyance toward her friends. No, Jude will not benefit from these insights. But I most certainly do – not in the sense of having learned a valuable life lesson, but in affective terms. Through the pleasures of comprehending (see Solomon 5), both myself (via my mother) and the narrative, I have gained what Feldman Barrett would call a deposit to my "body budget" (Feldman Barrett 82).

Comprehension is itself rewarding, then. But the rewards go beyond understanding story and extend to the issue of my involvement in it – what I have termed the mystery of emotion. In comprehending Jude's lack of illusions, and the denial of Jude, I came to organize my re-collected feelings about certain life events a little differently. That difference has proved meaningful for me. And because meaning can be very affecting, Jude's relatively mild musings, seeming like the milder expressions of my mother's thoughts in the lead up to major episodes of rage, have contributed to the formation of a new emotional stance toward my mother and myself. It is not vastly different from the stance I had already adopted. But it is, nonetheless, different. It is different because I have broadened my perspective-taking to include perspectives relevant to the construction of Jude's suffering. If Jude can be understood, so can my mother, and so too can I – as the child caught within the abnegating effects of her denial, and more lately, as woman caught within similar configurations because inequality persists and I am facing the same feared redundancy of being a woman in middle age.

Contemplating Australian Literature

In turning our attention, as readers, to the matter of what it is to be a mature Australian woman, Charlotte Wood has, with her novel *The Weekend*, made a significant contribution to Australian literature. Issues of equality are particularly significant for a nation that sees itself as middle-class and egalitarian, and Wood's novel persuasively shows us some of the ways in which we fall short of these aspirations.

There are many ways in which inequality operates in our society. The inequalities experienced by Indigenous Australians pose a significant problem for our country and the individuals thus impacted. Although *The Weekend* does not address this issue, it does offer insights on inequality that may be applied more broadly. In this respect, I rely on Armstrong's observations on the role of patterns in the formation of thought when I say that similar patterns in terms of outcomes and effects happen along lines of race, ethnicity, and culture. Outcomes like those articulated in the experiences of Wood's characters are not unique to issues of gender and age. Indigence and vulnerability (Adele), manipulation and exploitation (Jude), rebuttals of value in the face of success, with those rebuttals based on the individual's failure to "properly" perform their social role in accordance with their identity category (Wendy), can result from situations of inequality besides gender.

This is not to say that inequality is measurable on the same terms across social groups and cultures. But identity categories have emotional values attached to them, and our feelings about identity may sometimes prevent us from seeing a given situation for what it is when it is unjust. What the outcomes of *The Weekend* highlight regarding Jude, Wendy, and Adele, is the potentially limiting effect of social norms and expectations on the lives of individuals. Yet as much as they shape outcomes, normative values shape our reaction to unjust outcomes too. Norms, after all, are like blinkers – they can limit our vision. The impact of identity categories is of course relevant and still need to be taken into account, but when we identify the situation (poverty, vulnerability, disregard) independently of the normative values that apply to identity categories like gender, age, race, and ethnicity, we may gain insights we might otherwise overlook.

For Australian writers and scholars, the significance of this comes down to the questions we ask ourselves on key issues of equality. Using insights drawn from Wood's novel, we might ask ourselves, for example: Are there ways in which normative beliefs lead our society to downplay or discount the achievements of Indigenous people and culture? And do such beliefs impact our writing as scholars and creators of Australian literature? I think the answer is probably yes in both cases, but in saying this I am not undertaking a critical evaluation of any specific material. My point here is that I came to these questions via Jude's experience: Wood's finely drawn expression of the effects of inequality is highly thought-provoking. Such contemplating affects need not be limited to the novel's subject matter. The questions Wood's novel pose stand up to scrutiny on wider issues deeply relevant to Australian society and culture.

Conclusion

The interpretative capacity of emotion as a concept, brought within the intimate realm of thought as affect, has enabled my reading of *The Weekend.* Reading stimulates thinking, with the thinking that is provoked through the nested intimacies of grammatically established points of view likely to stimulate affects that in turn come to be organized under the concept of emotion. Perspective-taking is the means by which we feel emotion for ourselves as much as others: we take a perspective or stance – a seemingly objective stance – toward our subjective selves, and we feel for ourselves. When our internal realizations pertain to others, we no doubt feel for these others a little differently – with that difference marked by an awareness that we do not occupy both positions (of perceived and perceiver). It may be that identification sometimes obscures the distinction and I find myself moved to tears out of pity for myself, or I might experience feelings of elation through the memory of comparable happy events, via the perspective offered through the other. Empathy is no doubt something that is complicated by degrees of identification – we must recognize ourselves in partial terms, after all; but sometimes the part seems closer to the whole when reading moves us.

Works Cited

Armstrong, Paul B. *Stories and the Brain: The Neuroscience of Narrative.* Johns Hopkins University Press, 2020.

Barrett, Lisa Feldman. *How Emotions Are Made: The Secret Life of the Brain.* Pan Books, 2018.

Carroll, Joseph. "An Evolutionary Paradigm for Literary Study." *Style*, vol. 42, no. 2-3, 2008, pp. 103–425.

Damasio, Antonio. *The Strange Order of Things: Life, Feeling, and the Making of Cultures.* Pantheon Books, 2018.

Forgas, Joseph P. "Feeling and Thinking: Summary and Integration." *Feeling and Thinking: The Role of Affect in Social Cognition*, edited by Joseph P. Forgas. Cambridge University Press, 2000, 2001, pp. 387–406.

Frow, John. *Genre.* Routledge, 2006.

Frow, John. *Character and Person.* Oxford University Press, 2014, 2016.

Genette, Gérard. *Narrative Discourse.* Trans. Jane E. Lewin. Oxford: Basil Blackwell, 1972, 1980.

Genette, Gérard. *Narrative Discourse Revisited.* Trans. Jane E. Lewin. Cornell University Press, 1983, 1988.

Miller, D. A. *Jane Austen, or the Secret of Style.* Princeton University Press, 2003.

Solomon, Robert C. "The Philosophy of Emotions." *Handbook of Emotions*, edited by Michael Lewis, Jeanette M. Haviland-Jones, and Lisa Feldman Barrett. The Guilford Press, 2008.

Storey, Robert. *Mimesis and the Human Animal: On the Biogenetic Foundations of Literary Representation*. Northwestern University Press, 1996.

Tomasello, Michael. *Becoming Human: A Theory of Ontogeny*. The Belknap Press, 2019.

Wood, Charlotte. *The Weekend*. Allen & Unwin, 2019.

Zajonc, Robert B. "Feeling and Thinking: Closing the Debate Over the Independence of Affect." *Feeling and Thinking: The Role of Affect in Social Cognition*, edited by Jospeh P. Forgas. Cambridge University Press, 2000, 2001, pp. 31–58.

4 Affective Narratology, Cultural Memory, and Aboriginal Culture in Kim Scott's *Taboo*

Francesca Di Blasio

Indigenous literature has always played a vital role in the reconstruction of Australia's colonial and postcolonial history. It has contributed to illuminating the perspective of those who were dispossessed of their land and culture, and to shaping cultural memory (Di Blasio "*We Are Going* by Oodgeroo Noonuccal"). The role of the avant-garde First Nation writers of the past century was crucial. Through autobiographical novels (Doris Pilkington), drama (Jack Davies), and poetry (Oodgeroo Noonuccal and Kevin Gilbert), they narrated the Aboriginal version of events, and re-created a sense of cultural belonging. The new century has generously recorded voices that have continued and innovated within this tradition, giving it new and inexhaustible political and poetic strength. Among those voices are Alexis Wright, Melissa Lucashenko, Kim Scott, Tara June Winch, Tony Birch, and Claire G. Coleman. All of their writings are a meaningful contribution to the continuous remaking of a shared cultural memory for the country (Brewster 2015). This chapter deals in particular with Kim Scott's most recent novel, *Taboo* (2017), a text of great intensity that offers a lucid view of the past, present, and even future of Australia.

The first part of my discussion focuses on various theoretical perspectives on emotions that converge in my analysis of Scott's work. My *modus operandi* is to situate these theoretical views within a dialog that is perhaps eclectic and even "unorthodox," but which will hopefully lead to some interesting conclusions. In general terms, the word "emotion" can be considered paradigmatic for this investigation. Here, the term is understood in a broad sense, as a relational dynamic that is both physical and psychological, affective and cognitive, individual, and collective. Therefore, my critical perspective is not strictly understood as "cognitive theory," nor as a rigidly applied "affect theory," but these critical orientations will offer interpretive clues, as they are induced to interact with each other. They will also work synergistically with other theoretical perspectives (i.e., with "cultural memory studies" and with Martha Nussbaum's philosophical stance on "poetic justice") and reflections on the ethical value of esthetic emotion.

Theorein: Emotion from a Theoretical Perspective

First, it is worthwhile establishing the theoretical framework within which I will analyze *Taboo*. I have already noted that the concept of emotion, intended in a broad sense, is crucial to my argument. In the considerations that follow, this concept is linked to various issues. The first concerns the specificity of literary discourse. By offering many possible "representations" of the world, literature is endowed with a special, transformative power, which is at the same time "mimetic and imaginative" (Locatelli 2003, 8). Representing reality as transfigured by imaginative power, literary discourse is able to trigger special and specific responses in its users. In fact, it not only stimulates the critical function, but also activates an empathic response. By making up stories that are always different and never definitive, stories that captivate while using defamiliarizing devices, literature provides a form of knowledge that isn't taxonomic or "scientific," but which still yields knowledge that is effective and compelling. Literary worlds may be provisional or "unsubstantial," but their composite effects on readers are real. At once cognitive and emotional, they also trigger ethical, interrelational, and intercultural knowledge.

Critics coming from very different orientations, from philosophy to cognitive science, have recognized the positive role of this emotional component. Emotion is considered a source of knowledge and interaction, and this overturns the consolidated bias of the Western tradition to see it as "detrimental to both judgement and moral conduct" (Locatelli 2017, 77). Emotions are thus freed from the gray zone of mere impulsiveness, and become a repository for precise cognitive and relational power. Anchored to this insight, the critical perspective adopted here allows for a dialog between three different orientations in the theoretical reflections on emotion, making use of their potential elements of synergy and continuity, while backgrounding more oppositional features.

The reflections of Martha Nussbaum, Patrick Hogan, and Brian Massumi, to which I wish to refer, are rooted in different theoretical and philosophical perspectives. But in the analysis that follows, they will be situated in a critical dialog that underscores a specific feature of each: the ethical and collective role of emotions stemming from literature in Nussbaum's view; emotion as a subjective experience, and at the same time a relational "engine," in Hogan's cognitive perspective; and the "bodily" features of Masumi's affect theory, which situates emotional responses in the *space* of a relation, in the physical world more than in a subjective conscience.

In *Affective Narratology: The Emotional Structure of Stories*, Patrick Hogan focuses on the role of storytelling in triggering emotional responses, and elaborates on mankind's passion for storylines:

> Human beings have a passion for plots. Stories are shared in every society, in every age, and in every social context, from intimate personal interactions to impersonal social gatherings. This passion for plots is bound up with the passion of plots, the ways in which stories manifest feelings on the part of authors and characters, as well as the passion from plots, the ways stories provoke feelings in readers or listeners. Less obviously, but no less importantly, the structure of stories and even the definition of the constituents of stories are inseparable from passion as well.
>
> (Hogan 2011, 1)

Even what we already know takes on a different nuance when it is "emplotted" (i.e., when it becomes part of a narrative). This is a feature of literary discourse used to compelling effect in Scott's books, always suspended between fiction and reality. In the "Afterword" to *Taboo* (283), Scott tells readers that: "Although this is a work of fiction, it touches on real events, people and landscape." Different ways of articulating a story, its "subtleties" (Hogan 2011, 20), as Hogan calls them, provoke different emotional responses. Even if it is virtually impossible to systematize these diverse responses – since literature cannot be conceived as "data" in any conventional sense – such subtleties are relevant, especially when we consider emotional response as a cognitive process: "Millennia of storytelling present us with the largest body of works that systematically depict and provoke emotion, and do so as a major part of human life" (Hogan 2011, 17). Both in an intradiegetic perspective and in relation to readers' response to the texts, these observations are of paramount importance for exploring and explaining the role of storytelling in Scott's book. In fact, the reader "responds" to the specific and captivating story that is narrated in the novel; likewise, within the novel, characters are engaged in their own process of making sense, also at an emotional level, of the story they are experiencing.

Massumi's perspective draws on Deleuze and Guattari (1980, 2003) to propose a model of emotional interaction in which "affect" is opposed to "emotion," the latter being consistent with individual interiority. Affect, on the other hand, locates itself in the physical space of interaction, and can be considered a "zone of indistinction" between thought and action (Massumi, 2014). This emphasis on physicality is relevant for my analysis, because I will focus on the centrality of space/ place, and of certain material objects, in the way *Taboo* articulates the dynamics of emotional response. What Stephen Ahern says about affect theory proves useful to my hermeneutical hypothesis:

> Affect theor[y] signal[s] that there may be something more at stake than what concerns the individual as a self-determining entity, investigating moments of connection whose import exceeds what is often assumed; that such moments entail an experience laden with private meaning only, one in service of a consolidation of psychic identity or of spirit transcending the physical. The revolutionary insight of affect theory is to turn such individualism on its head, insisting on the relational rather than atomistic basis of all things.
>
> (Ahern 9)

This circumstance of interconnectedness somehow dwells in the realm of the "rhizomatic." In fact, according to Deleuze and Guattari, the rhizomatic model is perceived as oppositional to the arborescent, tree-like model, characterized as vertical and hierarchical, and by the duplicity and unopened continuity between its roots and trunk/crown. The "rhizomatic" is non-hierarchical, multiple, heterogeneous and connected, creative, and planar. In being so, it is the perfect theoretical counterpart to the idea of subjectivities engaged in cultural interaction [with their fellow humans], whether they live inside or outside the pages of a book; likewise, it fittingly represents interaction with the physical world, in the *hic et nunc* as in the time remembered and/or an uncannily haunting memorial past.

Ahern suggests that:

> To grasp the import of the protagonist[s]' struggles to govern their errant passions is to see that what's playing out demonstrates the

most fundamental insight of affect theory: that no embodied being is independent, but rather is affected by and affects other bodies, profoundly and perpetually as a condition of being in the world.

(Ahern 5)

Another central point in my analysis of Scott's novel deals with the *ethics* of emotion, in a line of continuity that goes back to Romantic esthetics and stretches forward to encompass Martha Nussbaum's work. Nussbaum's perspective leads us back again to the importance of stories: "emotions, unlike many of our beliefs, are not taught to us directly through propositional claims about the world, either abstract or concrete. They are taught, above all, through stories" (Nussbaum 1998, 226). In Nussbaum, the focus on the subjective quality of emotion returns: "Emotions contain an ineliminable reference to me, to the fact that it is my scheme of goals and projects. They see the world from my point of view" (Nussbaum 2001, 52). What is remarkable, however, in her philosophical position, especially as expounded in *Poetic Justice* (Nussbaum 1995), is the idea that the emotions aroused by stories influence behavior (i.e., that they have ethical value and consequences).

Literature is then a great catalyst for the emotions, and at the same time it sharpens our sensitivity to the world of the other, in a way that is neither prejudicial nor casual. This articulates in the reader an emotional response that is also defined in ethical terms, and according to parameters that are at the same time an identification with the other, and differentiation and autonomy. Emotional responses to narrative promote and cultivate the dynamics of an empathic response, as opposed to what happens with the "economic mind," which is blind "to the fact that human life is something mysterious and not altogether fathomable" (Nussbaum 2001, 433). This empathic response also nurtures the sense of an ethical response, to promote the "poetic justice" that is realized in the interaction between "literary imagination and public life." I will now go on to argue that the aspects of *Taboo* most related to the memorial scene, in the private as well as the public sphere, appear particularly consistent with this theoretical position.

Situating Kim Scott's *Taboo*: Place, Memory, and Empathy

Taboo (2017) is both a novel deeply rooted in the land that hosts the fictional scene and an "on the road" story. The physical space is experienced and represented as a journey or *process*. It is the fifth in a series of novels mingling fact and fiction, and comes after *Benang: From the Heart* and *That Deadman Dance*, among others. Some critics have observed how, rethinking Australian contemporary history in the light of Scott's literary production, these three novels offer more than a glimpse of the subsequent phases of that very history, from the frontier wars, to assimilation policy, to reconciliation – the latter the context of *Taboo*. This novel addresses the cultural confrontation with a difficult past, while trying to create newly established connections in the present, and for the future. This is well symbolized by the momentous episode at the center of the novel (i.e., the collective) and official event of the opening of a Peace Park on the site of a massacre of Indigenous people in the nineteenth century. In this respect, it functions as a powerful tool in the creation of a shared cultural memory, as defined by Aleida Assmann. In "Memory, Individual and Collective," Assmann focuses on the relevance of both individual and collective memory in political analysis, and investigates the close relationship linking the one to the other. This seems to be the case with Scott's novel, which preserves and transmits individual memory (intended as the cultural memory of a specific subject, but also the memory of a specific moment or episode). In so doing, the novel contributes to the creation of a collective memory, and ultimately to a sense of collective identity, that relies on this shared cultural memory (Di Blasio "(Post)Colonial History").

A polyphonic novel, *Taboo* features a clear-cut, well-rounded protagonist, presented by the narrator in the opening pages:

> There must be at least one brave and resilient character at its centre (one of us), and the story will speak of magic in an empirical age; of how our dead will return, transformed, to support us again and from within. (7)

Young Tilly is precisely this sort of character. From beginning to end, she is at the center of a story that revolves around a group of Noongar people traveling to the small Western Australian town of Kepalup for the opening of the Peace Park. The memorial site was conceived by the local community to commemorate an episode that had happened several generations before, a massacre of Noongar people by white landowners. The area had been considered taboo ever since the massacre, and no Noongar had been back there in a long time. Dan Horton is the owner of the land on which the massacre took place; his late wife, Janet, was very involved in the Peace Park project, and Dan is trying to honor her memory by getting involved himself, and by extending a welcome to the Noongar who are coming to visit the site. On the occasion of the opening, and throughout the narrative, these and other people gather and visit the land, thus breaking the taboo, and engaging in a journey of self- and reciprocal discovery. Among them are the oppositional and yet hard-to-tell-apart twins Gerald and Gerrard, who are relatives of Tilly. Gerald is on parole, but in prison he engaged in a process of reconnection with his Indigenous roots. In fact, another inmate, Jim Coolman, Tilly's father and Gerry's relative, now dead, "had been running 'culture classes', 'workshops'; whatever you wanted to call them" (14) and Gerry is now able to speak "language" (i.e., the Wirlomin language) as one, fundamental, form of reconnection with his own culture:

> It was true what people said: every old one left a hole in the world when they died, when they took language with them. That old language was a world itself, and one by one the words let you in. But individuals who could connect you to it, re-introduce you, they were necessary too. (14)

The main character, Tilly, a young and troubled woman, is the daughter of a white mother and an Indigenous father. Both deceased, they were in an abusive relationship. In her childhood, Tilly went through the experience of being a foster child, even to the Hortons, for a short period of time whose memory she lost. Reclaimed by her mother, she was raised estranged from Indigenous culture, and for her, as well as for others, reconnection to her Noongar roots is a journey that threads through the narration. Other characters populate the fictional world, from Doug, Dan's son, an abusive parole officer, to Wilfred, the Noongar artist who is the creator of a work of art, an "object," which is central to the critical perspective chosen in this essay.

In fact, in the case of Wilfred's creation and as a general rule in the novel, the special physicality of bodies, places, and objects in the making of the story contributes not only to represent the ineffable, but to make it emotionally available. The very act of visiting a taboo place conveys the sense of going beyond, of transcending the norms. In doing so, individually, collectively, and as a multicultural community, all the characters are facing history, and this also means facing themselves, their fears and ghosts, in an uncanny but necessary journey in space and time, and also in cultural difference and interaction. Places and objects, in this general frame of reference, play a pivotal role as catalysts of emotional responses, in the characters both collectively and individually, as well as in the readers.

As Scott notes in his "Afterword," many literary genres are represented:

> *Taboo* is a novel. It exists in a tradition of stories-in-print and this
> author chose to proceed in what might be called a trippy,
> stumbling sort of genre-hop that I think features a trace of
> Fairy Tale, a touch of Gothic, a sufficiency of the ubiquitous
> Social Realism and perhaps a tease of Creation Story. (283)

Most certainly, "ubiquitous Social Realism" is evident in Taboo's
unmitigated portrayal of the poverty, marginalization, neglect, addiction, and violence that are part and parcel of the fictional world.
But there is certainly much more than that, and that very fictional
world expands way beyond this merely realistic feature.

Starting from its opening sentence, "Our hometown was a massacre
place," *Taboo* gives the physical place, and its emotional and collective
implications, a central value that is preserved across the following
pages. In them, the physicality of places and the materiality of objects
hold a particular emotional value, performing a consequential narrative function, capable of influencing and orienting meaning. The
evocative vigor of these images endowed with a special "materiality"
becomes one of the significant features of the novel, and one of the
bases of its poetic power in terms of empathy and healing. The objective correlative of this central role of the "material" is the land, not
only the one inhabited by all the characters, but also the one traveled
through: the land is the object of an emotional relationship articulating
itself in many different shapes. All of these shapes, though, seem
connected to an ancestral past, that needs to be confronted, from each
and every side. The centrality of space, and of the *physical* place, is on
show from the very beginning. The space, that is also the place of a
collective and individual trauma, and of a past and present experience,
reveals itself not just as a background that hosts the events that are
being narrated, but as a protagonist *per se*, and takes on a cardinal
narrative function. Cultural memory originates and develops *inside* a
physical space, which is charged with an emotional overtone. This is
the case with the place of the massacre, which arouses emotions of
pain, fear, and sorrow, and it is the case, more in general, within the
novel as a whole where landscapes are concerned. Physical descriptions of places, especially of natural places, are never plainly illus-
trative; the quality of the represented space is always emotionally
connoted, as in the episode of the kangaroo suddenly appearing in the
vibrant landscape the protagonists move through (231). This is a

"relational" and "animated" landscape, made of the recurrent objects that give substance to the narrative: sticks, leaves, sand, water, creatures of flesh and bones, even the wire fence. All of these elements participate in sustaining the emotional nuances of places and in building up interconnected relations in the story. Moreover, it is worth anticipating how the scene of the kangaroo peeping in and out of sight recalls and redoubles the progressive revealing itself to sight of a skeleton in another episode. As I will show in the following pages, these situations represent the core of the emotional "physicality" of the novel.

Scott gives his own commentary on the fictional world in the "Afterword," which provides interpretive cues that potentially expand the narrative beyond its merely "material" confinement:

> *Taboo* offers a little band of survivors following a retreating tide of history, and returning with language and story; a small community, descended from those who first created human society in their part of the most ancient continent on the planet, provides the catalyst for connection with a story of place deeper than colonisation, and for transformation and healing. (287)

These are words filled with many hermeneutical suggestions. There is the reference to language, as the element of its revitalization is central to the novel.[1] The reference to narration, to the actual presence of a story as a relevant item that is able to reconstitute the sabotaged identity of a whole community, evokes what has been said previously on the power of stories in emotional and relational terms. Likewise, the physicality of the place, a place which itself has a history that makes it meaningful, is unequivocally associated with the idea of "transformation and healing."

Focus, Objects, and Emotional "Landscapes"

Another interesting aspect of the novel, and one which contributes to my critical reading, is the quality of the narrator's voice. In some ways, the text features an omniscient narrator, firmly holding all sides of the story in its hands, an impression enhanced by the circularity of the narrative. The structure of the story is in fact circular, as it opens and closes with the same episode, a "revealing" accident that introduces a very significant object. This object is also an artifact, and one of the symbols of the oneiric magic realism that is typical of the novel as a whole; this artifact is literally made up of all the objects that have critical and emotional relevance within the novel. We will explore this further in a moment. Keeping the focus on the circular structure of the narrative, it can be said that it turns the story told within the "boundaries" of the novel into a sort of long flashback, in turn interspersed with even earlier narrative segments. Circularity obviously projects the story into the realm of myth, thus echoing the narrator's voice in the opening passage: "death is only one part of the story that is forever beginning" (3). The omniscient narrator, then, appears to be in control of all these elements; yet, this stark voice is also capable of articulating an interesting form of reticence. The narrator offers us a view of the story that tends to subtract certain elements, or to present them in partial, visual sequences reminding readers of live Handycam footage. These "deictic" visual sequences are arranged by accumulation rather than as the result of an overview. It is as if the narrative voice itself saw the scene at the same time as both the characters and readers, thereby emotionally enhancing our grip on what is offered up for all of us to see.

The relationship that is formed between the text and the reader is obviously very important for establishing emotional dynamics. More than once, the text addresses the readers directly ("A bystander – perhaps even you, dear reader [...]" (5); "Come close. Closer" (6)), summoning them through the use of the conative function of language, inviting them to draw near, to make decisions, to be involved, to participate, also emotionally, in what is happening. At the scene of the accident, which then duplicates itself, circularly, at the end of the novel, these fascinating textual dynamics are first established (5–6). This reiterated episode reinforces the centrality of the spatial setting, which is portrayed as part of a vitalistic and emotional paradigm. It also features a "multilayered" place. In fact, Kepalup is suspended between fiction and reality; it is the place of trauma and "recovery"; it has the uncanny quality of taboo and its overcoming, through the reconstruction of a shared cultural memory (*sensu* Assmann). These passages epitomize the narrative technique described previously, and gradually reveal an emotionally connoted landscape. They also represent the event from different points of view, as the writing is articulated from different physical and emotional distances. The reader is on the spot, as well, and is emotionally involved in what is going on, and in the expectation of some turn of events ("an explosion"? (5)). Eventually, a woman and a man emerge from the truck involved in the accident, and in the first version of the story, to be narrated again in the final part, nobody knows who they are (with the possible exception of the now-reticent narrator). But there is a third figure on the scene, a mysterious "entity" that is endowed with great symbolic strength and triggers curiosity:

> Imagine a figure sitting in a deep and rapidly draining bath: head and shoulders appear, then the upper torso, knees... In the trailer, beginning with the dome of a dark skull, a figure is being revealed. (6)

In this last passage, the echo of the "revelation" of the kangaroo's body mentioned can be considered as one of the many subtle textual traces alluding to certain symbolic intra- and inter-textual motifs. Earlier on, the invitation to "Come close. Closer" features both an emotional and a spatial dimension; this twofold proximity implies emotional interaction as connected to physicality, thus confirming the hermeneutical hypothesis expounded in this essay. In fact, by encouraging closeness, the narrator activates an emotional dynamic in the readers' response to *this* specific story. The echo effect created by the circular repetition of the first scene at the end of the novel reinforces this sense of "coming closer," like a vortex sucking us in toward its center. The third figure that was in the truck, and that emerges from the falling heap of wheat, gradually reveals itself as an anthropomorphic, artistic, and symbolic creature; it is identified as a skeleton, and a very singular one. It is made up of all the elements of Noongar country: stone, bones, "polished timber," "woven grass," "brightly colored feathers," "cords of sinew," "neatly knotted fishing line," maybe human hair, and "even fencing wire." And "[i]ts whole being is a smile" (7). This figure is a palimpsest, and at the same time a rhizomatic being, in the sense given previously; it is the creative result growing from the special "thingness" of this novel. It is the epitome of this story, of the history in the background, and of cultural memory. As an artifact, it stands for the semiotic double of the novel itself. Like the novel and the story it narrates, it is the catalyst for everyone's gaze. The complex and enticing physicality thematized in the novel coalesces in this figure, and it is no coincidence that it emerges from a truck that just a bit earlier in the book was compared to a "breaching whale" (5). The figure of the whale could in fact be an intertexual reference to one of the traditional stories recovered and narrated in the Wirlomin Noongar Language and Stories Project website, *Mamang* (2011). In this story, a human figure enters a whale, and within it continues to wander across the sea, and to tell the stories of his people, until both are able to find the land in which each will continue to exist according to their own form and shape.

A vital and historicized landscape and the *things* it is made of thus become the elements of a new creation, capable of involving, both emotionally and narratively, the protagonists of the fictional world, and their readers. Through the interconnectedness of stories, physical space and its dislocated and relocated objects are experienced as elements in a cultural memory that functions emotionally, or affectively, "moving from body to body across time and space" (Rogers 2019, 210). This is the "magic" the novel speaks about "in an empirical age" (7). The rhizomatic roots of Noongar storytelling, which are grounded in space and place, get revitalized in a new segment of an endless story.

Conclusion

Taboo combines individual and collective cultural memory with the materiality of space and place, and with the land and its "objects." In so doing, it activates a dynamic of interaction, at the intra- and extra-textual level, of an emotional kind. Although they can be delineated in different ways according to different theoretical perspectives, here emotions, understood in a broad sense, have been dealt with as forms of interaction that are exquisitely intrinsic to literary discourse, and endowed with a cognitive power that is part and parcel of human relations. The fictional world of the novel fuels this emotional potential, and the physical and artistic figure of the skeleton becomes the epitome of this dynamic. The physicality of places and objects participates in the emotional dimension, and is filled with it. In this way, the fruition of narrative objects and places becomes a repository of cultural memory. And from the dynamic perspective of these emotions, this cultural memory is shared, or at least made shareable. Objects and places are therefore not coldly material, or opposed to the human, but become emotional, cognitive, and participative devices.

Note

1 Language revitalization is also at the core of the Wirlomin Noongar Language and Stories Project promoted by Scott: http://wirlomin.com.au/.

Works Cited

Ahern, Stephen, ed. *Affect Theory and Literary Critical Practice. A Feel for the Text.* Palgrave, 2019.
Assmann, Aleida. "Memory, Individual and Collective." *The Oxford Handbook of Contextual Political Analysis*, edited by Robert E. Goodin and Charles Tilly. Oxford UP, 2006, pp. 210–224.

Brewster, Anne. *Giving this Country a Memory*. Cambria Press, 2015.

Deleuze Gilles, and Felix Guattari. *Millepiani*. Castelvecchi, 2003 (1980).

Di Blasio, Francesca. "We Are Going by Oodgeroo Noonuccal. Aboriginal Epos, Australian History, Universal Poetry." *Le Simplegadi*, vol. 17, no. 19, 2019, pp. 119–127.

Di Blasio, Francesca. "(Post)Colonial History, Personal Stories. Indigenous (Auto)Biographical Writing at the Intersection between History and Literature." *Textus*, vol. 32, no. 2, 2019, pp. 47–60.

Hogan, Patrick Colm. *Affective Narratology: The Emotional Structure of Stories*. University of Nebraska Press, 2011.

Locatelli, Angela. *La conoscenza della Letteratura/The Knowledge of Literature II*. Sestante, 2003.

Locatelli, Angela. "Emotions and/in Religion Reading Sigmund Freud, Rudolph Otto, and William James." *Writing Emotions: Theoretical Concepts and Selected Case Studies in Literature*, edited by Ingeborg Jandl, Susanne Knaller, Sabine Schönfellner, and Gudrun Tockner. Transcript Verlag, 2017, pp. 77–96.

Massumi, Brian. *The Power at the End of the Economy*. Duke UP, 2014.

Nussbaum, Martha. *Poetic Justice: The Literary Imagination and Public Life*. Beacon Press, 1995.

Nussbaum, Martha. "Narrative Emotions. Beckett's Genealogy of Love." *Ethics*, vol. 98, no. 2, 1998, pp. 225–254.

Nussbaum, Martha. "The Literary Imagination in Public Life." *Hard Times*, edited by Fred Kaplan and Sylvère Monod. Norton, 2001, pp. 425–450.

Rogers, Jamie Ann. "Invisible Memories: Black Feminist Literature and Its Affective Flights." *Affect Theory and Literary Critical Practice. A Feel for the Text*, edited by Stephen Ahern. Palgrave, 2019, pp. 201–217.

Scott, Kim, Woods, Iris, and the Wirlomin Noongar Language and Stories Project. *Mamang*, with artwork by Jeffrey Farmer, Helen Nelly, and Roma Winmar. UWA Publishing, 2011.

Scott, Kim. *Taboo*. Picador, Australia, 2017.

5   Finding Voice: Cognition, Cate Kennedy's "Cold Snap," and the Australian Bush Tradition

Lisa Smithies

Introduction

"Voice" is a term used often in creative writing, academia and literary criticism, yet it is a term that is difficult to define precisely. As writers, finding a good voice in which to tell a story is one of the best tools we have "for creating a believable world with believable characters" (Gebbie 17). The voice "belongs to both the body and mind" and it "bridges our internal and external worlds" (Karpf 4). Finding a voice is a key aspect of the writing process. For the writer, voice feels like an enigmatic entity that emerges as a piece of writing develops.

This chapter seeks to unpack the elusive idea of voice; specifically, how we move from what is essentially a biological process—of air moving through flesh—to what we mean as writers when we talk about voice. I argue that, for the creative writer, voice does not simply refer to the individual expression of a writer; nor is it simply a narrator's voice, or a character's voice. It is, in part, all of these things, but can also be something more ephemeral. Using a cognitive lens, I aim to study "voice" as a living entity in writing and reading; with a focus on the bush tradition in Australian short fiction. Examining Cate Kennedy's short story "Cold Snap," in relation to several cognitive capacities—paralanguage, inner space, and hypostasizing—I explore the notion of literary "voice" as potentially more than a metaphorical moniker.

Finding Voice in "Cold Snap"

Voice is a sound made as air, expelled from the lungs, causes the vocal cords to vibrate. This sound is amplified by the vocal tract (throat, mouth, and nose) to create a "person's recognisable voice."

The "articulators" (tongue, soft palate, and lips) modify this sound to form words (TVF). In her book, *The Human Voice: The Story of a Remarkable Talent* (2006), Anne Karpf writes:

> The voice is one of our most powerful instruments, lying at the heart of the communication process. It belongs to both the body and the mind [...] It bridges our internal and external worlds [...] It's a superb guide to [...] another person's vitality and authenticity... (4)

How we use our voice is determined by our cultures, societies, and esthetic preferences. The dimensions of voice can be altered (intentionally and unintentionally) by the physicality of the person speaking. The "lungs, abdomen, throat, lips, teeth, tongue, palate, and jaw [...] unite to make a voice" and "tiny changes" in any one of these "can entirely alter mood and meaning" as it is received by a listener (Karpf 3). Voices can be trained (in acting and singing, for example), they have accents, and they use different languages, dialects, and vocabularies; all of which influence how that voice is "heard" by others. Voice is fundamentally linked to identity, to emotion, to what it is to be human. Karpf contends, you "can't really know a person until you have heard them speak" (4). Whenever we open our mouth to speak, "our voice is doing something terrifyingly intimate—leaking information about our biological, psychological, and social status. Through it, our size, height, weight, physique, sex, age and occupation, often even sexual orientation, can be detected" (10). Literary theorists have long discussed voice in texts, but this use of "voice" has been largely metaphorical. I contend that connections may be drawn that show how the physical phenomenon of voice can be transferred to a page in more than merely metaphorical terms.

Arguably, the most influential definition of literary "voice" is the one made by Gérard Genette in *Narrative Discourse*, where he examined the syntax of storytelling, pointing out "the way in which the narrating itself is implicated in the narrative" (31). Put most simply, in Genette's model, "the narrated story can be analysed under three separate headings: *temps* (tense), *voix* (voice), and *mode* (mood)" (Fludernik 619). Monika Fludernik notes that "in the reception of Genette's work, and in his own contrasting of focalization and person, the formula of "who sees" (focalization) versus "who speaks" (voice) has become the hub on which narratology is supposed to turn" (620). However, she emphasizes that voice "cannot be simply reduced to the question "who speaks," or to the subcategory person" (620). For Fludernik, the separation of *speaking* and *seeing* into separate domains is problematic. She instead proposes the term "narrativization" to account for the ways in which "readers read narrative texts" (623), as this term acknowledges that readers "project real-life parameters into the reading process and, if at all possible, treat the text as a real-life instance of narrating" (623). In this projection of "real-life parameters," cognition is key. Fludernik contends that in reading "it is a useful strategy to hypostasize the existence of a narrator figure who is telling us the story and whose presence and existence seem to be vouchsafed for by the stylistic features of authorial diction" (623). This notion of hypostasizing (to treat something that is abstract as if it is real) is central to our reading and writing experiences. If the voice feels real, the story feels real.

Author Amanda Lohrey describes the "flick-through test" she applies when choosing to buy a book: "I open the book at random and I am looking to see, and hear, if the voice is there for me, if it compels my attention. Sometimes I think in terms not of favourite stories but favourite voices. The best have a quality of song, of incantation" (6). She argues that, in the art and craft of storytelling, the "primal thing is the voice" (6). Voice gives stories a "capacity to weave a spell" (7). As author Maria Tumarkin describes it, voice is "a unique combination of many different characteristics [...] it is never one thing or one quality." Hence, in this analysis, I will not attempt to extract one "thing" from Kennedy's short story "Cold Snap" and label it "voice." Genette argued the story and the telling could be separated, but my feeling is that, in this story at least, voice is inextricably linked to storytelling itself. The story is the *telling*.

Cate Kennedy's short story "Cold Snap" won the Australian *HQ Magazine* short-story competition in 2001 and has been published in several versions since, including as "Black Ice" in *The New Yorker* (2006) and as "Cold Snap" in her collection *Dark Roots* (46–57). It is told from the first-person perspective of Billy, a child who lives a harsh life with his single father in the bush. Billy traps rabbits to sell to a local dog owner as pet food – he is saving to buy a bike. Over the course of the story, Billy has several interactions with the lady who moved in up the hill: she has come from the city, with grand plans to gentrify her little bush property. As the story progresses, it becomes clear that Billy is not like other kids. He is ridiculed by his teacher, the other kids, and the lady as: "backward," "special," and "a bit of local colour." While Billy struggles to fit in with local society, he is perfectly adapted to this bush setting; and when he realizes the lady has been secretly killing old Gum trees in order to improve her view, he sets a trap and she is killed when her car loses control on the black ice.

Since the earliest Australian short stories,[1] the bush has been represented as "hostile, full of nameless terrors, [and] ultimately destructive" (Lord 3); the children lost to the bush in these stories, were rarely found. "Cold Snap" plays both with and against these traditions. The Australian short story developed since the nineteenth century, as seen in historical anthologies such as Mary Lord's *The Penguin Best Australian Short Stories,* Carmel Bird's *The Penguin Century of Australian Stories,* and Laurie Hergenhan's *Australian Short Story.* With these developments, the form captured moments of contemporary Australian life, with uniquely Australian voices.[2] These stories captured the cadence of our lived experience, echoing voices with a developing sense of national identity, and embodying many different experiences of what it is to be Australian. Within this historical tradition, Henry Lawson is the most recognizable of *The Bulletin* writers of the 1890s who cemented the "bush realism" style, which dominated the Australian short-story form well into the twentieth century (Clunies Ross). This "unpretentious, unadorned prose style" successfully married Australian style and content, to tell stories that "existed in a recognisably and uniquely Australian landscape, and spoke in an authentic Australian dialect" (O'Neill 22). The authentic, unpretentious Australian style evident in "Cold Snap" harks back to bush realism, but this story addresses contemporary concerns in the Australian bush. Billy's relationship with the bush is the heart of "Cold Snap." Within this story, the dynamic between the lady, the child, and the natural environment is a troubled one, with wider social and political implications. And, as such, it fits with the Australian short-story tradition of using a uniquely Australian voice to examine our contemporary preoccupations; in this case, it leans toward the emerging area of eco-fiction, which addresses our often-problematic relationship with our natural world (Fetherston).

"Cold Snap" begins:

> When I go down to check my traps, I see the porch lights at that lady's place are still on, even though it's the morning now. *That's an atrocious waste of power*, my dad says when I tell him. His breath huffs in the air like he's smoking a cigar. The rabbit carcasses steam when we rip the skin off, and it comes away like a glove.
>
> *Skin the rabbit*—that's what my mum used to say when she pulled off my shirt and singlet for a bath. Mr Bailey gives me $3 for every

rabbit to feed his dogs. I take them down in the wooden box with a picture of an apple on it. At the butcher's, rabbits are $2.50 but Mr. Bailey says he likes mine better. I've got $58 saved. I want to get a bike.

(Kennedy 46)

In these opening paragraphs, a child's voice is semantically recognizable in "my dad says," "my mum used to say," and "I want to get a bike." There is a sense that he lives in a harsh world; skinning rabbits efficiently is not something usually associated with a child. There is also a sense of pride in the way he recounts how he gets a better price for his rabbits than the butcher offers, but, in general, there is little emotion in the way Billy tells this story. Billy is not a neurotypical child. His condition is never named, but it is clear that he does not comprehend the significance of the comments made by those around him. His lack of understanding is mocked by others on several occasions. For example, there is an interaction with the lady and her partner, Roger, where Billy narrates: "They both laughed and laughed and Roger said, *Well, it looks like the light's on but there's no one home.* Which was wrong. They were both home and they'd turned the lights off by then" (52). Billy is not so much an unreliable narrator, as an overly-reliable one; he reports dialog verbatim, as well as events, without the color of emotion or metaphorical significance. As Billy himself does not always understand, it is left to the reader to discern the true meaning (and subtext) of characters' words and actions. Readers must use various cognitive abilities to comprehend the significance (in terms of plot, characterizations, etc.) of what Billy is narrating; playing what he understands against what he does not, in order to appreciate that the *real* story is more complex than the one he *tells*.

While this chapter focuses on other cognitive capacities, it is pertinent to note the role of Theory of Mind here: this is our cognitive capacity to *read* other people – their thoughts, their words, their intentions (Zunshine 10). While many animals have the ability to understand the behaviors and relationships of others within their species, only humans seem to have an elaborate multi-leveled theory of mind. It is crucial to how we understand the positions of both characters and narrators. We can (almost automatically) track what one person might think, plus we can understand what a second person might think about what the first person thinks, and also what a third person might think about what the second person thinks about what the first person thinks, and so on. Billy does not seem to have this ability, but the story relies on the reader shifting positions in this way to understand the true meaning of the story that Billy is telling us. In making these shifts, in "Cold Snap" the reader must also supply the emotion that Billy himself seems incapable of articulating.

Many aspects of a text contribute to its sense of voice, such as characterization, dialog, point of view, tone, etc. However, when examining voice in "Cold Snap," the boundaries between these begin to blur, as all seem to contribute to the sense of voice in this story. When I talk about voice, here, I am not talking about speech literally (overt speech and texts are clearly different things); however, there are crucial correlations in the way that both speech and text *give voice* to lived experience. Cognition is central to these correlations. Cognitive linguistics takes an "experientialist position" on human understanding, believing it is "determined by our organic embodiment and by our individual and collective experiences" (Geeraerts and Cuyckens 57). In other words, cognition and language are inseparable from each other and inseparable from all our bodily and worldly experiences. Thus, voice, in the many ways we use it (both metaphorically and literally) is intrinsically linked not just to language, but also to body and mind. And further to this, in literature, voice "is a language performance—always social, mediated by experience, and culturally embedded" (Sperling and Appleman 71). So, when we read voice in a text like "Cold Snap," we cannot help but bring to bear our meaning-making apparatus (our cognition) and all its experiential, social, and cultural complexities.

Paralanguage – What Billy Does Not Hear

A large part of our comprehension of spoken language comes not from the words themselves, but from the ways in which they are said. For example: in a bar, someone says, "Do you want to step outside?," it is the vocal delivery that determines whether this is an invitation or a threat (Karpf 59). Delivery is context. This is paralanguage—tone, pitch, tempo, facial expressions, loudness, body language, etc.—which affects how we judge the words being said, and it "can be more important than language itself. For paralanguage doesn't just support words but gives them life" (33). Furthermore, "what we hear, or think we hear, […] is affected by judgement, volume, and other factors […]. In other words [what we hear] is subjective" (35). As listeners, we are constantly switching emphasis between placing importance on the words and/or the delivery (60). In particular, intonation (tone and pitch) draws attention to certain information; it tells us which words are important and gives us the emotional signals to correctly read potentially ambiguous statements (35). Emotion and language comprehension are inextricably linked; however, Billy does not seem to have the ability to recognize intonation, or its emotional significance. Many parts of the brain are responsible for marrying language and inflection in order to process what Karpf calls "vocal emotion" (59–61), but the right hemisphere plays the most significant role in allowing us to understand the "emotional aspects of voice" (61). It gives us the ability to "distinguish the voice of a happy person from a sad one, and intuit the metaphorical meaning of a phrase rather than its literal one. [...] Labelled our 'emotion processor', the right hemisphere allows us to assign social and emotional significance to speech melody" (58). The right hemisphere is responsible for "judgements based on a speaker's tone of voice rather than [the] meaning" of the words alone (58). Like Billy, "people with right-hemisphere damage often have difficulty understanding context and connotation [...] they also have problems detecting inconsistency between words and tone, and find it hard to distinguish between lies and jokes [...] metaphor and irony pass them by" (59). Karpf likens it to a painter "unable to use colour" (59). I am not implying that Billy has a particular kind of brain damage, merely that he has much in common with these descriptions. He seems to lack the emotional processors that give spoken words their *true* meaning.

Paralanguage makes obvious the inextricable connection between language, body, and mind. But drawing attention to paralanguage presents a paradox for the textual analysis of voice – how can we call it "voice" when, physically, a text is only words on a page, whereas paralanguage is a living, breathing phenomenon? One view of literary voice is that it is an illusion produced by the craft of creative writing; yet, when I read (and when I write) there is a distinct sensation that someone or something is actively *speaking*. This may be related to our inclination to "hypostasize," as Fludernik described it. Hypostasizing can be tied to the cognitive linguistic idea that language and all our bodily/worldly experiences work together to make meaning and knowledge. Just as our voice can bridge "our internal and external worlds" (Karpf 59); we take what we *know* to a text and hypostasizing allows us to treat the voice of others within that text as *real*. Through hypostasization, we not only have the ability to inhabit Billy's inner world, but to also understand his external world (through his eyes) in a way that he cannot. That is perhaps because the layers of meaning we gain from paralanguage may be something we look for, even if it is not present. Like Hemingway's famous iceberg metaphor, this short story reveals just the tip of the real story, on the page, and the reader is left to recognize the multilayered story underneath Billy's narration.

Our ability to hypostasize also correlates with another cognitive notion – that of inner language and inner space. We are well acquainted with the concept of the "mind's eye," but not so familiar with the idea of the "mind's ear." When a writer writes (and a reader reads) they tap into an established propensity for "inner language." This inner language is part of the ongoing background noise of our minds known as "inner space"; in other words, what is going on in the mind at any given time. Inner space has been examined in several scientific studies, with participants carrying around a beeper that goes off randomly throughout the day; they then "describe properties of their mental contents at each random beeper signal," using various methods (Lœvenbruck). These studies found that "inner space incorporates our cultural, social, and linguistic environment"; and cognitive neuroscientist Hélène Lœvenbruck suggests that, "on average, approximately a quarter of our inner space consists of inner verbalisation, the rest is made up of images, emotions, sensations and unsymbolised elements" (ibid). This background melange of inner language, emotions, and sensations are part of the way we make sense of our everyday experiences; and it is something that a fictional narrative like "Cold Snap" taps into. We are readily able to hypostasize (and recognize "voice") when we read, because of this already-present meaning-making melange. This, combined with our predilection for paralanguage, means we actively *hear* the voice in "Cold Snap."

Inner speech is not subject to the same constraints as external speech – physiological constraints, like breathing and tongue movements; or social constraints, like turn taking, etiquette, or the need to be understood. For example: "when we speak aloud, we need to take breaths between fragments of speech, as speech only occurs during expiratory phases. Because it is not subjected to these physiological constraints, inner speech is accelerated compared with overt speech" (Lœvenbruck). Furthermore, inner language is not "only physically shortened with respect to overt speech, it can also be syntactically condensed, or left elliptical" (ibid). Therefore, inner language often has an abstract quality. This internal linguistic abstraction, again, offers comparisons with "Cold Snap": it is particularly evident in the first-person narration, which uses ellipses (all that is not said) and occasionally leans toward a stream of consciousness mode; for example, when Billy narrates in run-on sentences with little punctuation.

Putting together these ideas—paralanguage, inner language, and hypostasizing—allows for a conceptualization of literary voice that makes *natural* sense to the mind. Paralanguage helps us deal with linguistic ambiguities and to attribute emotional significance to utterances. While inner language exemplifies our ability to allow the linguistic to sit comfortably alongside more abstract aspects of meaning-making, such as "images, emotions, sensations and unsymbolised elements" (Lœvenbruck). Through hypostasizing, the reader (and writer) can take on a story's voice to build a kind of mental persona, not just of the narrator or characters, but of the story itself. Indeed, in "Cold Snap," it is not just the narrator, or characters that have a voice, but the story itself – a *storyvoice*, if you will. As with David Herman's storyworlds, through textual cues and inferences, storyvoice allows a reader to reconstruct a kind of voiced entity. As I will now discuss, for Kennedy, this voice is not just about who speaks – it is inextricably linked to story construction.

Giving Voice to the Australian Bush

About a third of the way into "Cold Snap," a kid from school ridicules Billy:

> One day a boy at my school who works at the feed supply told the other kids that we were so backward we didn't even have hot and cold running water at our place. He said, *It's like Deliverance down there with you-know-who.* I asked Dad what deliverance was and he rolled a cigarette and said why.
>
> (Kennedy 49)

The next time this child delivers chicken feed from the store to their house, Billy's father sets up the water heater so the child is badly scalded: "... and then there was a scream and the boy came running out holding his hands in front of him. They were bright pink like plastic. As the boy ran past, my dad called, *Don't forget to tell your friends.*" (50) This scene was fundamental for Kennedy in finding the voice of this story. As she says, she had a "moment of confidence" while she was writing that scene, when she knew exactly what had to come next:

> [Nature is not...] out to hurt us, it's just itself. [...And Billy is...] operating on behalf of the natural world. [...Nature] is remorseless and here is this small agent of nature who contains within him that same remorselessness. You are never going to win against that kind of coldness.
>
> (McVeigh)

While it was the father's actions that elicited Kennedy's revelation, this lack of warmth is fundamental to the story and the way it is told – it is evident in Billy's poor emotional comprehension, in the matter-of-fact manner in which he narrates the story, in his actions, and in his bush environment. This is the Australian bush in winter – harsh, cold, and unforgiving. The children in our earliest short stories were at the mercy of the bush, as seen in the nineteenth-century "Lost Child" tales, like Marcus Clarke's "Pretty Dick" (Lord 61–76). Billy is not lost, however; he is an active agent of the bush. He works to re-store balance to his natural world, ridding it of both the feral rabbits and the "civilizing" influence of the lady.

Like the bush, as Kennedy describes it, Billy is "not relentless, or out to hurt us"; he is just himself. Billy may not always understand what others around him are saying, but he has great empathy for his en-vironment. He is not cruel; he makes sure the rabbits are trapped in a humane way, so that they do not needlessly suffer. At times, he even imagines himself as a rabbit, getting down low into the rabbit tracks around the lake:

> I made myself small as a rabbit and moved through them on my soft scrabbly claws. I saw everything different then. Saw the places they sat and rested, the spots where they reached up with their soft noses and ate tiny strips of bark from the bottoms of the river willows.
>
> (Kennedy 47)

At other times, Billy floats above, surveying the landscape; as when he finds the dying trees. Here, he says: "When I looked real hard I flew up again and saw them from the top and the dying ones made a kind of line down to the lake all the way from the lady's house on the hill to the shore. Then I came back down onto the ground, and I saw how it was" (54). Billy acts as an embodiment of the bush. He has the ca-pacity to be in this environment on multiple levels and to really see just *how it is*. In Kennedy's description of finding the voice of this story during the writing process, Billy and the bush became intertwined and inseparable. So, with "Cold Snap," when we examine the voice of Billy, we are examining the voice of the bush as well. This is the point of the story – Billy is the bush (and vice versa).

Kennedy says a writer's voice is not so much to do "with your au-thority or expertise, it's to do with your instinct for language and your intent to honour the voice of the character you're inhabiting and not intruding […] you are invisible." That way, she says, "you can focus on the prize and let the character direct plot […because] plot is the vehicle in which your character is driving your story" (McVeigh). In this way "character is to voice is to theme is to plot is to story" (King 249). Thus, the voice of "Cold Snap" is not simply the voice telling the story, but integral to the story itself.

Conclusion

This story creates an experience in the mind of the reader that indeed, like our physical voice, "belongs to both the body and mind" and "bridges our internal and external worlds." This experience, as described through Billy, again illustrates the cognitive linguistic view that cognition and language are inseparable from each other and inseparable from all our bodily and worldly experiences. The reader looks for clues for how to interpret what this *storyvoice* is telling them – linguistically, socially, and culturally.

This discussion does not distinguish between voice-driven, narrative-driven, or any other type of storytelling in short fiction. Nor does it endeavor to speak for all short fiction, Australian or otherwise. However, when Kennedy discusses her process, I see correspondences with my own – finding that "voice" is fundamental to finding the meaning of a story. Genette argued that the story and the telling could be separated, but my feeling is that, in "Cold Snap" at least, the story is the *telling*. Voice gives this story a quality we can believe in, because a living dynamic exists between our everyday use of our physical voice and the writer's use of voice in a text. Voice is a living, breathing entity, both in life and on the page, thanks to our underlying cognitive capacity for paralanguage, inner language, and hypostasis.

Notes

1 Acknowledgment is necessary that these stories were written and told on country with an extensive, pre-existing, indigenous storytelling tradition. The intention here is not to overlook indigenous contributions to Australian short fiction, but rather to focus on the Australian bush tradition, which is inherently non-Indigenous.

2 Again, it is important to acknowledge that Australian voices are more diverse than those discussed in this chapter. The 1960s and 1970s, in particular, saw a reappraisal of "ideas about nationhood and culture which had evolved around the bulletin in the 1890s" (Clunies Ross), with writers challenging traditional bush realism tropes. Recently, more diverse Australian voices have emerged within Australian short fiction; with Maxine Beneba Clarke's *Foreign Soil* (2014) and Tom Cho's *Look Who's Morphing* (2009), just two examples transforming notions of an "Australian voice." Similarly, Ellen van Neervan's *Heat and Light* (2014), Jeanine Leane's

Purple Threads (2011), and Tony Birch's *Common People* (2017) are examples of Indigenous writers reclaiming storytelling and transforming the short-story form. This chapter does not intentionally omit this diversity; however, it lies outside the scope of this discussion.

Works Cited

Clunies Ross, Bruce A. "Some Developments in Short Fiction, 1969-1980." *Australian Literary Studies*, vol. 10, no. 2, 1981, pp. 165–180.

Fetherston, Rachel. "Greener Pastures and Tangled Gums: The Rise of Australian Eco-Fiction." *Overland*, 2016. https://overland.org.au/2016/12/greener-pastures-and-tangled-gums-the-rise-of-australian-eco-fiction/.

Fludernik, Monika. "New Wine in Old Bottles? Voice, Focalization, and New Writing." *New Literary History*, vol. 32, no. 3, 2001, pp. 619–638.

Gebbie, Vanessa, ed. *Short Circuit: A Guide to the Art of the Short Story*. London: Salt Publishing, 2013.

Geeraerts, Dirk, and Herbert Cuyckens. "Introducing Cognitive Linguistics." *The Oxford Handbook of Cognitive Linguistics*, edited by Dirk, Geeraerts and Herbert Cuyckens. New York: Oxford University Press, 2007, pp. 53–89.

Genette, Gerard. *Narrative Discourse*. Oxford: Blackwell, 1980.

Herman, David. *Story Logic: Problems and Possibilities of Narrative*. Lincoln: University of Nebraska Press, 2002.

Karpf, Anne. *The Human Voice: The Story of a Remarkable Talent*. London: Bloomsbury Publishing, 2006.

Kennedy, Cate. "Cold Snap." *Dark Roots*. Sydney: Scribe Publications, 2006, pp. 46–57.

King, Zoe. "But What If Your Character Won't Talk to You?" *Short Circuit: A Guide to the Art of the Short Story*, edited by Vanessa, Gebbie. London: Salt Publishing, 2013, pp. 248–251.

Lœvenbruck, Hélène. "What the Neurocognitive Study of Inner Language Reveals About Our Inner Space?" *Épistémocritique: littérature et saviors. [electronic resource]*, vol. 18, 2018. https://epistemocritique.org/what-the-neurocognitive-study-of-inner-language-reveals-about-our-inner-space/.

Lohrey, Amanda. "An Introduction." *Cracking the Spine: Ten Short Australian Stories and How They Were Written*, edited by Julie, Chevalier and Bronwyn Mehan. Sydney: Spineless Wonders, 2014, pp. 5–6.

Lord, Mary. "Introduction." *The Penguin Best Australian Short Stories*, edited by Mary, Lord. Melbourne: Penguin Books, 2000, pp. 1–23.

McVeigh, Paul. "Cate Kennedy Interview." July 19, 2015. https://paulmcveighwriter.com/2015/07/19/cate-kennedy-interview/.

O'Neill, Ryan. "How to Read an Australian Short Story." *Cracking the Spine: Ten Short Australian Stories and How They Were Written*, edited by Julie, Chevalier and Bronwyn Mehan. Sydney: Spineless Wonders, 2014, pp. 21–29.

Sperling, Melanie, and Deborah Appleman. "Voice in the Context of Literacy Studies." *Reading Research Quarterly*, vol. 46, no. 1, 2011, pp. 70–84.

TVF. "Anatomy and Physiology of Voice Production." 2017. https://voicefoundation.org/health-science/voice-disorders/anatomy-physiology-of-voice-production/understanding-voice-production/.

Zunshine, Lisa. *Why We Read Fiction: Theory of Mind and the Novel.* Columbus: Ohio State University Press, 2006.

6 On Waiting Upon: Speculations by an Australian Novelist on the Experience of Writing a Commissioned Novel

Sue Woolfe

Introduction

After writing a best-selling second novel, originally published as *Leaning Towards Infinity: How My Mother's Apron Unfolds Into My Life*, I had writer's block. In casting around for a solution, I found that neuroscience both indicated what the brain might be doing during creativity, and helped me find a way out of my paralysis. (Woolfe ix–x). Many years later, the writing of a commissioned fifth novel, the subject of this chapter, became such a struggle that I turned again to neuroscience, and realized that the commission had not emboldened me, but inhibited me. In this chapter, I trace through the lens of neuroscience the effect of inhibition on my cognitive processes and the final creation. I ask what, if any, implications this research has for other creators who may, by anticipating readers, inhibit their creativity.

Amabile cited Dostoevsky, who told a friend that being commissioned by a Russian publisher to write a novel with a fee in advance was "hellish torture," even though he was not given guidelines but merely had to produce something wonderful (Amabile, Hennessey, and Grossmann 14). Often readers have told me that they assume a novelist writes to communicate with them, but for some of us, that is a misunderstanding. When I interviewed fellow-writers, I found the fear of readers who were judgmental was not an uncommon theme: Helen Garner spoke of hearing an inner, sneering voice that is "pre bad review"(Grenville and Woolfe 69); Peter Carey found bad reviews "devastating" because he had already anticipated them (ibid 39); and Kate Grenville went further, saying that "getting into the critic or review state of mind" made her so timid that the writing "gets strangled with sheer caution" (ibid 104).

Amabile, researching in the late years of the twentieth century and the early years of this one, expressed uncertainty whether the reason for the anxiety that can affect creativity was "affective or cognitive" (Amabile, Hennessey, and Grossmann 22). Liane Gabora's more recent work led me to the speculation that it may be cognitive; anxiety about a critical readership may cause a difference in the way the brain of the author actually works, and the creator may wittingly or unwittingly control the working of the brain, in order to avoid criticism. In this chapter, I trace how I unwittingly "strangled" myself and by what cognitive means, the latter to suggest that the inhibition was not solely caused by emotion. I also discuss the solution to creative inhibition that the neuroscience indicates.

A Case That, in Order to Create, the Creator Uses Distinctive Cognitive Processes

It is necessary to explain my usual thought processes as a fiction author when I have not been commissioned. All through my 20s, I wanted to devote my life to writing fiction, but had been given the strong impression in my undergraduate and masters' years that fiction authors had knowledge of the book before they wrote it, and intended their effects. This seemed a commonsense assumption – otherwise, how would a coherent work come about (Woolfe 17)? But by my early 30s, I had never had an idea for a novel, and I feared that if I waited for it, I would wait a lifetime. In a last attempt to become an author, I traveled to a country where I knew no one and shared no language with its people, so that if it turned out for the worst, I could fail in secret. With nothing left to do but start my new life, I had no idea where to begin. On the first day of writing, I sat twisting my pencil, my mind in idle. Later I was to find out how vital that idling was. Immediately, my mind began behaving in a most odd way. I had had a vague notion that I would write down memories, but my mind suddenly seemed to present images that had never happened, but which often moved me to tears – tears over something I had simply made up. I wrote in apparently disconnected fragments. I was compelled to keep writing by a strange and preposterous intimation that I could almost hear the world weeping, and it might be my job to comfort it.

The disturbance I felt has been noted by scholars as part of the creating process. Liane Gabora wrote that creativity is often thought to originate with the generation or awareness of a sense of incompletion, which may arise spontaneously, or slowly over the course of years, and be of trivial or of worldly consequence. This sense of incompletion may be described as a chaotic cognitive state, and be accompanied by a lingering feeling that compels the exploration and expression of ideas ("Honing Theory: A Complex Systems Framework for Creativity" 42).

Scribbling fragments by hand since then has always worked for me, scribbling anything that came to mind and worrying later how it might cohere and what it might amount to. This became my method, and what I have done ever since. In the scribbling, I am not exactly waiting for anything. I am aware that the following may seem overly poetic or fanciful, but my method was affirmed by Heidegger and Matisse. Heidegger makes a distinction between "waiting for" and "waiting upon," distinguishes between "calculative" thinking, where one "waits for" and "meditative" thinking (Heidegger 46), and fears that "calculative thinking may one day be accepted and practised as the only way of thinking." (56) In his own words, "In waiting upon, we leave open what we are waiting for." (25) Heidegger constructs a dialog between a Scientist, a Scholar, and a Teacher:

Scientist: Yet if we wait, we always wait for something.
Scholar: Certainly, but as soon as we represent to ourselves and fix upon that for which we wait, we really wait no longer.
Teacher: In waiting we leave open what we are waiting for. (68)

When the scholar asks for explanations, the teacher replies: "Because waiting releases itself into openness." (68)

What I am waiting upon is what the scribbling wishes to become, if it wishes to become anything at all. In Matisse's words, admittedly about visual art but which has great resonance for me, I seem to be waiting upon "the desire of the line, where it wishes to enter, where to die away" (Hotere 1). I have found, with every novel I write, that eventually the scribbling shows its "desire." This "waiting" upon the "desire of the line" is reflected in the following recent neuroscientific observations.

Over the last 50 years, there has been increasing neuroscientific evidence for two kinds of thinking processes. One well-known model of cognition is the "Geneplore model" (Finke 388) which, simply put, proposes an initial generative phase of the creating process in which the creator uses insight, intuition, and incubation. This is followed by an exploratory phase in which these ideas are analyzed and manipulated, when the creator's mind zigzags between the two in what Kelly called "a creativity cycle" (Woolfe 62).

About the initial, generative phase: in 1962 Mednick found that, whereas most people have what he termed steep associative hierarchies so that a given stimulus evokes only highly related memories, creative people have distinctively flat associative hierarchies so that a given stimulus evokes not only highly related, but also remote memories (Gabora and Ranjan, "How Insight emerges in a Distributed, Content Addressable Memory" 27). In a 1975 landmark experiment, Colin Martindale found that creative people achieved this by spontaneously lowering their brain activity (Woolfe 88–89). In later years, neuroscience would observe this more precisely as lessening the most goal-driven, predictive, value-laden conscious part of their brain activity. In so doing, creators have more mental resources left for heightened sensitivity to subliminal impressions. Dietrich saw it as a redistribution of resources:

> Creative abilities are enabled by a process that tends to deactivate the pinnacle of human evolution, the pre-frontal cortex... From the moment you stop thinking about the creative task consciously, a massive redistribution of the brain's resources is under way....

> (Dietrich 154)

Here it is necessary to explain that the prefrontal cortex, the pinnacle of human evolution, is responsible for doing Heidegger's "calculative" thinking, as well as housing our values and beliefs.

Where the "massive redistribution" of resources moves to are our conscious memories and those subliminal experiences which are stored across many locations in the brain. Gabora again:

> It seems sensible that the more stimulus features one attends to, or is sensitive to, the more memory locations the current instant of experience gets stored to; that is, the more widely distributed the activation function. ("The Beer Can Theory of Creativity" 157)

There is a further implication here: if creators, even when they are creating, but just going about their ordinary life, are commonly in the state of the lowered brain activity that Martindale observed, they may have more mental resources left to take in an unusually high number of stimuli, but also they may be forming enriched representations of their existing knowledge and experiences. New perspectives on old experiences may come spontaneously to light, or new connections may be made between previously unconnected pieces of knowledge. Ranjan and Gabora stress that memories are "distributed and content addressable" ("How Insight Emerges in a Distributed, Content Addressable Memory" 22), which is critically important for creativity, because any stored information that shares features (for example, crispness, or a particular shade of pink, or a particular sound pitch) are encoded in overlapping neurons, and therefore stimuli that activates one neuron, activates a multitude (ibid 22). Gabora likens it to "getting a bite on many fishing rods at once, and when you reel them in you get a fish that is a mixture of the characteristics of the various fish that bit" ("Towards a Theory of Creative Inklings" 162). This then, is the "inkling" I wait upon, which may or may not arrive.

Nancy Andreasen, in her fMRI studies of creatively successful people in the United States, comments that they must be running on neural processes that are "enlarged or enriched." She depicts extraordinary activity in the mind once creativity has begun:

> It is as if the multiple association cortices are communicating back and forth … simply in response to one another. The associations are occurring freely. They are running unchecked… Initially these associations may seem meaningless or unconnected. I would hypothesize that during the creative process the brain begins by *disorganizing,* making links between shadowy forms of objects or symbols or words or remembered experiences that have not previously been linked…many of which may seem strange or implausible. Out of this disorganization, self-organization eventually emerges. (77)

About the exploratory phase, the Geneplore second type of thinking: after scribbling some 70,000 words in fragments, for a critical mass seems necessary, all my previous fiction manuscripts have given me an "inkling" that something has shifted, that the reason for all this work has become present. I dare not ask for anything more. Once this has happened, I have then used the second type of thinking, and found commonalities between the fragments, commonalities of setting, mood, character, incidents, even emotive words. The accumulation of these commonalities reveal what John Briggs called the "themata."

Briggs, a literature professor who read neuroscience in the early years of this century, speculated that creators keep a set of sense nuances in their minds which never come to consciousness, but which tend to "draw out" data that is relevant to the creation. He termed them "themata," enduring ideas that for the creator have esthetic and thematic qualities – for example, that the true order of things is hierarchical, or that the structure of reality is in constant flux (46). Themata give creators a concrete feeling for the world, often with a visual component, and attune them to see the world in certain fundamental ways, putting them in contact with what he called their "data of great complexity" logged in their minds from childhood. The creator may be trying to find a meeting place between the nuances of personal themata and universal laws, and senses this meeting place as "truth." This, Briggs suggests, is the meaning behind Emily Dickinson's declaration that "my country is truth" (Briggs 82).

The "themata" ultimately have encoded in them the underlying purpose for the creation, and so a work comes to seem to the artist a microcosm of the universe as he or she uniquely feels it to be (102).

Despite the late entry of the themata into the process, or more likely, because of this late entry, the themata give structure and style to the entire creation, and so the author finds the "desire of the line" within the scribbling.

For me, finding the themata after years of travail and uncertainty, is a moment infused with bliss, and it is why I court the terror and anxiety of writing fiction, and perhaps why some others do. Once I recognize the "themata," I oscillate between analytic thinking as well as generative thinking, to sculpt the manuscript to them. Gabora calls this sculpting phase "honing" ("Honing Theory: A Complex Systems Framework for Creativity" 41).

A Case for Considering the Reader as a Co-creator

Gabora takes the idea of the themata emerging much further than Briggs, suggesting that the re-structuring of the work according to the themata actually *heals* the creator. A creation comes together, in Gabora's terms, because of:

> the self-organizing, self-mending nature of a worldview....Through the creative process, the creator assimilates experiences and memories into a more cohesive worldview and expresses or manifests this worldview.
>
> ("The Recognizability of Individual Creative Styles Within and Across Domains" 352)

Moreover, because it is distinctive in style and meaning, the worldview brought about by this procedure can be discerned by others. Gabora, O'Connor, and Ranjan further expand:

Since the raw experiences one has are to a degree unique, and there are individual differences in the manner in which individuals assimilate and express their experiences, a worldview is expected to develop a characteristic structure, and the creator's outputs are different expressions of that structure.

Gabora and her colleagues refer to the creative style that expresses it as "fingerprints" (357).

If the creation, distinctive in style and meaning, develops in this way out of the creator's "truth" or worldview, then the worldview in the creation may be discerned by others, with the potential to heal them. It seems that readers and audiences may sense authenticity. In early experiments conducted by Henderson and Gabora, authenticity ratings between viewers of performed works were significantly positively correlated ("The Recognizability of Authenticity," 2527–2528).

Half-way through last century, Ernst Kris argued that the beholder of a creation is not passive, but re-creates in his or her mind:

> Communication lies not so much in the prior intent of the artist as in the consequent re-creation by the audience of his work of art. And re-creation is distinguished from sheer reaction to the work precisely by the fact that the person responding himself contributes to the stimuli for his response.
>
> (Kris 254)

We know from the work of Rizzolatti on mirror neurons, first on monkeys and then on humans, that we all have a primitive communication system spread across important regions on both sides of the brain, so we share with each other a neural mechanism that enables a form of direct experiential understanding. Rizzolatti pointed out that "when people use the expression 'I feel your pain' to indicate both comprehension and empathy, they may not realize how literally true their statement could be" (Rizzolatti, Fogassi, and Gallese 60). So is it possible that some readers intuit in a writer's "multidimensional fingerprints" an echo of their own "gaps," their own unexpressed yearnings and their misgivings about themselves, their place in society and in life – their own sense of dissonance, their yearning for equilibrium? Might those readers share in some works the creator's "worldview," and deeply assimilate it?

Non-creators learn not to be creative; this premise has been tested many times through research study findings (Vint 1275). However, John Briggs said that everyone has a sense of their own creativity "in uncanny moments, as a fleetingly strong sense that a mix of different contours and feelings one has about the world must somehow go to-gether" (32). For the creator, these sensations are all-important. "For others, probably because of what Joseph Conrad in *The Nigger of the Narcissus* called 'the war-like conditions of existence,' these sensations become submerged and fragmented" (85), and people are carried along by "the way the consensual world perceives things" (33). If Briggs is right, perhaps this has implications for the teaching of creativity – not as a brain activity never experienced, but as a brain activity that might be, with help, remembered. Further research could be warranted.

Further, I wonder if it is possible that some readers intuit in a writer's "fingerprints" an "uncanny moment," a fleeting sense that disparate things might go together, an echo of their own sense of in-completion, their unexpressed yearnings and their misgivings, their sense of dissonance, their yearning for equilibrium? Might those readers share in some works the creator's "worldview"? Might the themata reflect also the readers' "truth" and their "data of great complexity"? And if creativity is in part about surrendering to the creation and allowing it to heal, might those readers also be co-creators? As Jane Tompkins wrote, a book that comes after the reader:

> lets me see my situation in a new way, and it will begin to re-form itself, take on different contours, become explicable, analysable [...]. Eventually, whatever the trouble is will lose its mystery and hence its power. It will become just another facet of your makeup that you recognize, understand, [...] (4). Tompkins says reading a book in this way is "spiritual or sacred" because it makes her feel light, clear-headed, joyful, loved and understood – in other words, she participates in it, and it heals her.
>
> (Tompkins 5)

A Case That the Creator, Fearful of Readers, May Choose, Wittingly or Unwittingly, Not to Use Distinctive Cognitive Processes

To come back to my experience of writing my commissioned novel; after 200,000 scribbled words, I stopped writing. I had experienced no hunch, no "inkling." By now it was November, seven months until the deadline. Nevertheless, I did what I always do: I typed up every word. I searched, not for the themata, for I wasn't so optimistic, but at least as usual for commonalities. I could find nothing.

In all the writing, I had not felt safe from judgment. This had nothing to do with the personalities of the people in the publishing house. It was entirely my worry about their expectations. In my previous manuscripts I had always been able to convince myself no one would ever read them. This time, always in the background had been a constant humming, like the humming of an air-conditioner: "I must please them! Will this impress them?" Perhaps wrongly, I had a deep conviction, the basis of which I am not sure, that they wanted from me a "charming" story, like my private, somewhat wry assessment of the set of short stories of mine they had recently published. What I longed to write was a novel that surprised me, that violated my own expectations.

I suspect my problem lay in the social implications of Martindale's "flat associative hierarchies." Martindale found in his previously mentioned 1975 word association tests, that the self-avowed "uncreative" people associated the word "table" with commonsense connections like "chair," "food," "desk," "cloth," and "leg." The "creative" people after spontaneously and intuitively lessening their brain activity as previously described, associated "table" with much more unexpected ideas such as "ocean" and "victory." Unexpected, imaginative, but also bizarre. That last word rankled me. Although the idea of creativity is theoretically admired, Barron in 1969 concluded that creativity requires "resistance" to socialization and Burkhardt argued that the creative individual must fight against society's pathology (Cropley 307).

All this leads me to speculate that a commissioned author anxious about readers' responses, or perhaps exhausted with resisting society's pathology, can wittingly or unwittingly inhibit her brain activities, disallowing the plundering of remote associations and the combining of new associations. She may intuitively know how to encourage the brain to revert to analytic thinking prematurely, so that "the fish" that is "caught" is not a fish the like of which the world has never seen, but just something ordinary, like a mullet. Indeed, Sowdon, Pringle, and Gabora speculate that an "idea monitor," a mechanism that evaluates ideas, might continually check "the output of idea generation processes… This suggests that individuals have the capacity for evaluation 'on tap' and can apply it to keep the generation in check" (Sowdon, Pringle, and Gabora 47–48).

Or as Dietrich wrote:

> There is a top-down or deliberate creativity mode that is strongly biased by top-down projections from the prefrontal cortex. These top-down influences tend to restrict the heuristic search function to more commonsense solutions so that the deliberate mode is

liable to yield creative insights that are more paradigmatic in type and rely on more close associations. (10)

To speculate further, can a creative person, usually using flat associative hierarchies, willfully decide instead to force top-down control of their brain activities, and create using their prefrontal cortex, the seat of our "calculative" thinking? Is this what I had done? That this choice may be possible for an individual seems to me to have implications for teaching people to resist limiting their creativity, and instead become more creative.

A Case for the Creator's Distinctive Cognitive Processes – In Practice

By now, it was January. The deadline was June. I could see that in the 200,000 words, because of the settings, characters, and multitudinous incidents, I could cobble together a set of short stories concerning the lives lived in an apartment building like the one I lived in, linked by a drama I dimly conceived about a concierge. I had admired such works, such as Jose Saramago's *Skylight* or Georges Perec's *Life: A User's Manual*. It would surely pass as a novel, perhaps even a charming novel. But this was Heidegger's "calculative" thinking. I knew intuitively that any skill I have uses Heidegger's "meditative" thinking.

On the first day of March, with three months to go, I came to a turning point: I had to throw away those 200,000 words. I had to start again. A few hours of sleep later I began in a new notebook, writing by hand again. That morning, as if suddenly given permission, a sense of incompletion opened up in me. Over 30 years of fiction writing, I had fought hard not to write what I most wanted to write: my bewilderment at my own past. I was tired of tricking myself, tricking others. Regardless of who saw, read, criticized, mocked, derided, condemned. On that day, heedless of anyone's approval or disapproval, I began to write for myself. The writing emerged in a grim, stripped-bare voice of taut sentences. The story of a child growing up in isolation with a very beautiful but violent mother. My own story.

By June, I had 90,000 words about my bewilderment which I did not intend to show anyone, and certainly not the publishers. I requested an extension. They removed me from their marketing schedule. I did nothing for a week or two. Emotionally exhausted, I was gazing at a photo of a child's cot in a state of Martindale's "lowered brain activity." I found myself groping toward a question I had never asked in all the years after that childhood: I had always asked, "Why did she hit me? Why didn't she love me?" At last, I asked, "What had gone wrong for her?" I was now at my "disjuncture," longing for "equilibrium." I found myself scribbling about hundreds of tiny, unremarkable, almost forgotten moments: the unexplained frequent catches in my mother's breath as if she was gasping, it seemed to my childish self, in horror; the frequent murmuring of incoherent, puzzling phrases when she drugged herself to sleep; her averted gaze out windows at an empty sky, the thousand-yard stare I have heard described of men who had seen the horrors of a battlefield; her trembling and then her fury when I asked questions, as children do, about her childhood, her mother – in all, I was experiencing the nudges of remote, normally inaccessible memories of a terrified, vigilant child suspecting throughout her childhood that something immense, unspeakable, secret, and ghostly was behind her mother's behavior, and that her life as well as our continuing life together depended on its secrecy. But there was about her also something endearing, pleading, something beseeching, as if she desperately wanted someone to know what was behind it all. And so, 40 years after her death, I began to understand what she had been telling me in code all along.

With mounting apprehension, a rumor came to my consciousness, a rumor I had heard early in life about my mother's horrific childhood. I wrote a letter: a letter came back: the rumor was true. The feeling I had was as if the world, previously racing by, had quietly come to a halt. It's an unearthly silence, the silence when the writing really begins. I picked up my pen. From then on, the book wrote itself, a book unaware of itself, unaware of readers, of publishers, unaware of anyone's expectations, unaware of my expectations, unaware of me, my duties, my responsibilities; the actual world became slippery, only a dream, as were my home, family, duties, responsibilities, life. The real world was the book, and where I now lived was in a "country of truth." Then I used analytical thinking, and with the "oscillating" of the "creativity cycle," I had at last a novel.

Conclusion

There is a weight of evidence that during the creation, a person uses distinctive cognitive processes in order to "create a new pattern on the fly that is more appropriate to the situation than anything that has even been input to the network" ("How Insight Emerges in a Distributed, Content Addressable Memory" 24), or as Gabora put it more colloquially in an address to Simon Fraser University, a person "pull(s) out of the brain something that was never actually there." This is made possible, it seems, by the creator spontaneously de-activating the prefrontal cortex to create new ideas in the generative part of the creative process. Only creators use this ability, unwittingly or otherwise, although, as previously stated, others could. The image of the cot for me had activated memories, or more precisely, had accentuated connections that I had never noticed before.

In the analytic part of the creative process, the creator uses the "calculative," analytic thinking commonly done by creators and non-creators alike, to piece the material together and eventually create a work that reflects their hidden, secret self. "Themata" emerge, that have both stylistic and thematic implications, with their "fingerprint." The resulting creation may haunt certain readers, who see in it a reflection of their own unrealized yearnings, and who may, like the creator, be healed by it.

I have speculated in this chapter that a commissioned creator, if fearful of exposure of his or her secret and bizarre self to a critical readership, may intuitively, wittingly or unwittingly, revert to a way of creating that is more controlled, or entirely controlled, by the prefrontal cortex, in order for his or her "worldview" to remain private. But if this happens, Gabora's research implies that the creation does not have the riches of our distributed, content addressable memories to enable it to cohere, or in other words, the "themata" with its influence on the themes and style of the work, do not emerge. The processes I describe, and my early fear of exposure to critical readers, may have implications for the training of creativity.

Works Cited

Amabile, Teresa, Barbara Hennessey, and Beth Ann Grossmann. "Social Influences on Creativity: the Effects of Contracted-for Reward." *Journal of Personality and Social Psychology*, vol. 50, no. 1, 1986, pp. 14–23.

Andreasen, Nancy. *The Science of Genius*. Plume, 2011.

Briggs, John. *Fire in the Crucible: Understanding the Process of Creative Genius*. Phanes P, 2000.

Alder, Hans, and Sabine Gross. "Adjusting the Frame: Comments on Cognitivism and Literature." *Poetics Today*, vol. 23, no. 2, 2002, pp. 195–220.

Cropley, Arthur. "Creativity in the Classroom: The Dark Side." *The Dark Side of Creativity*, edited by David Cropley, Arthur Cropley, James Kaufman, and Mark Runco. Cambridge University Press, 2012, pp. 297–315.

Dietrich, Arne. *How Creativity Works in the Brain*. Palgrave Macmillan, 2015.

Finke, Ronald. "Imagery, Creativity and Emergent Structure." *Consciousness and Cognition*, vol. 5, no. 3, 1996, pp. 381–393.

Gabora, Liane. "Towards a Theory of Inklings." *Art, Technology, Consciousness: mind@large*, edited by Roy Ascot. Intellect P, 2000, pp. 159–164.

Gabora, Liane. "The Beer Can Theory of Creativity." *Creative Evolutionary Systems*, edited by Peter Bentley and David Corne, Morgan Kaufmann, 2002, pp. 147–161.

Gabora, Liane. "Honing Theory: A Complex Systems Framework for Creativity." *Nonlinear Dynamics, Psychology and Life Sciences*, vol. 21, no. 1, 2016, pp. 35–88.

Gabora, Liane, Brian O'Connor, and Ranjan Apara. "The Recognizability of Individual Creative Styles Within and across Domains." *Psychology of Aesthetics, Creativity and the Arts*, vol. 6, no. 4, 2012, pp. 351–360.

Grenville, Kate, and Sue Woolfe. *Making Stories: How Ten Australian Novels Were Written.* Allen and Unwin, 1993.

Heidegger, Martin. *Discourse on Thinking.* Harper and Row, 1966.

Henderson, Madeleine, and Liane, Gabora. "The Recognizability of Authenticity." *Proceedings of the 35th Annual Meeting of the Cognitive Science Society*, 2013, pp. 2524–2529.

Hotere, Ralph. *The Desire of the Line.* Auckland UP, 2005.

Kris, Ernst. *Psychoanalytic Explorations in Art.* International Universities P, 1952.

Land, George. Youtube, https://www.youtube.com/watch?v=ZfKMq-rYtnc

Gabora, Liane, and Apara Ranjan. "How Insight Emerges in a Distributed, Content Addressable Memory." *The Neuroscience of Creativity*, edited by Adam Bristol, Oshin Vartanian, and James Kaufman. MIT P, 2013, pp. 19–43.

Rizzolatti, Giacomo, Leonardo Fogassi, and Vittorio Gallese. "Mirrors in the Mind." *Scientific American,* vol. 295, no. 5, 2006, pp. 54–61.

Sowdon, Paul, Andrew Pringle, and Liane Gabora. "The Shifting Sands of Creative Thinking: Connections to Dual Process Thinking." *Thinking and Reasoning*, vol. 21, no. 1, 2015, pp. 40–60.

Tompkins, Jane. "Deep Reading." *The Journal of the Assembly for Expanded Perspectives on Learning*, vol. 22, 2016–2017, pp. 1–5.

Vint, Larry. "3Cs: Creating a Culture of Creativity." *Design 2006*, International Design Conference, Croatia, 2006, pp. 1275–1284.

Woolfe, Sue. *The Mystery of The Cleaning Lady: A Writer Looks at Creativity and Neuroscience.* U Western Australia Publishing, 2007.

7 Performing a Neuro Lit Crit Analysis of *Specky Magee* in the Australian Health Context: Persuading Readers to Exercise

Rocío Riestra-Camacho

Introduction

Motivation to engage in exercise can be altered through exposure to others' experiences of physical activity, which need not be performed in our presence or even by actual people. Following this lead, I suggest that sports narratives can influence readers' attitudes, and ultimately their behaviors, around exercise. In particular, I argue that the Australian football novel *Specky Magee* (2002) would be useful in the context of "narrative persuasion in health," the field of study dealing with the persuasive effects of narratives on people's health lifestyles. This desirable project would combat the risks of a sedentary lifestyle and overweight, which the Covid-19 crisis has worsened. Not only is this particularly relevant to the Australian health context, where obesity already affects one-quarter of children (Australian Bureau of Statistics par. 1), but it also has precedent, since Australian football fandom has previously been successfully exploited in an intervention to tackle overweight (Aussie-FIT 5–7).

In this analysis, I offer a close reading of the potential of corporeal descriptions in *Specky Magee,* emphasizing the possible influence exercised on its readership by the characters' successful engagement in sport. *Specky Magee* is a third-person "Australian football novel" (McAdams 258) written by former Aussie Rules player Garry Lyon and children's book author Felice Arena. This novel, part of a larger series, centers on Specky, its protagonist and focalizer, and a passionate Rules player. Specky's family is unsupportive of his hobby, and upon finding a photograph of himself as a baby dressed in football clothes, he starts to wonder whether he is adopted. This leads him to research his football-loving biological father, and it is via this search that the narration pays homage to the protagonist's achievements by engaging readers in highly detailed descriptions of the movements required in this sport.

The first part of this chapter uses the literature on embodied cognition to explore how reading *Specky Magee* might be expected to activate the readers' motor system. The second part employs the literature on narrative impact to identify three pathways through which reading *Specky Magee* might motivate readers to engage with exercise: cognitive appraisal, empathy, and simulation. The last section looks specifically at research that has tested the links between reading about action, movement, or sports, and related behaviors.

The Neuroscientific Potential of Corporeal Descriptions in *Specky Magee*

Neuro Lit Crit is a comprehensive research field that is useful to analyze how these descriptions might affect young readers' motivation toward engaging in physical activity. The primary reason for this is that Neuro Lit Crit is defined as "the use of the cognitive neurosciences" to investigate "what underlying processes are activated when we read" (Vidal and Ortega 191–192). One of these processes is linguistic motor resonance, or the activation of areas in the human brain when reading about corporeal activities, specifically those parts that control movement. The motor resonances provoked by Specky Magee, in particular, could motivate readers to exercise. Engagement with physical activity is a crucial step to preventing and combating overweight and encouraging a healthy lifestyle in children.

Seeing others exercise is an excellent way to develop motivation for physical activity. According to the Embodied Cognition Framework or Grounded Cognition Framework, witnessing physical actions creates a resonance in the motor system of subjects. Motor resonances can be defined as changes in corticospinal excitability while observing actions performed by others. In other words, they reflect the activation of our own motor system upon seeing others move, and it has been shown that they play a role in increasing motivation to be physically active (Ross-Stewart 29–31).

In line with this model, there is a growing body of evidence that motor resonances need not be induced by direct observation of physical actions. Currently, neuroscientists are shifting their interest toward linguistically triggered motor resonances, or motor imagery: "the provocative idea that comprehending a linguistic description of an action might involve covertly recapitulating the type of action that it refers to, using some of the same brain systems that underlie the execution and observation of that type of action" (Kemmerer and González Castillo 57).

It is generally held that mirror neurons are responsible for the activation of relevant motor cortex areas. Although the existence of mirror neuron activity in humans has been questioned, recent studies seem to have confirmed it (Fuelscher et al. 2877). In linguistic motor resonances, neurons fire in the areas which would become active if the reader performed the action herself (Kemmerer and González Castillo 57).

Acknowledging that skepticism exists as to the scope of what mirror neurons can help us explain, these findings are pertinent to analyzing a salient characteristic of *Specky Magee*. In particular, the novel contains detailed descriptions about how to be a proficient player or "tips on improving your game" (Foster 127), with instructions to perform specific Rules movements correctly. The motor resonances provoked by these elements of *Specky Magee* could prompt Australian young readers to play football and exercise.

Even though any part of the body can be utilized in Rules, the main actions involved are kicking, handballing and running with the ball, and often jumping. Running is the most frequently described action in *Specky Magee*. Kemmerer and González Castillo report functional magnetic resonance imagery (fMRI) evidence that reading "running verbs engage[s] a leg/foot-related primary motor region" (67). A motor resonance will be evoked by reading running verbs at the opening of the novel, when the narrator describes the performance of one of Specky's teammates:

> No one could stop him [Danny Castellino]. He was as fit as a greyhound, and could run nonstop for an entire game. Robbo acknowledged Danny by spearing the ball directly on to his chest. It was a safe mark, but Danny didn't have the luxury of taking his time. He charged off towards the forward pocket area. (6)

Robbo and Danny are the main secondary characters in the novel. In this passage, the verb construction "charged off" not only activates readers' leg-related primary motor region, it also contributes to encouraging them to run thanks to the information surrounding this action. Firstly, a direct relationship is established between Danny's capacity to sprint fast and his body shape. The simile is clearly based on a correspondence between running and fitness, whether one interprets that slimness as a consequence or one of the causes of Danny's sprinting ability.

Apart from modeling endurance as a source of motivation, the ability to sprint supports the description of Danny as a tough and competitive player. The capacity to run is therefore presented as a successful trait, and in fact eventually provides Specky with an opportunity to take possession of the ball and perform his first "specky." Specky is the main character's nickname, as well as a famous mark in Rules that the narrator's words illustrate:

> With one giant leap, he was suddenly airborne. He propped his right knee securely between the shoulder blades of his pig-like opponent and catapulted his entire stretched-out body high above the players around him [...]. With arms outstretched, fingers well spread and eyes fixed on the ball, he was never going to drop it. (6)

An increase in physiological activity occurs with imagined movement in line with the vigor of the envisaged effort (Wilson et al. 422). The intensity of jumping conveyed by this passage contributes to a greater activation of the leg-related motor cortex region. Jumping high is not the only requirement involved in a specky, however. A player also needs to grab the ball in a specific sequence, and reading about the protagonist's performance here will induce activation of the arm and hand-related motor area of the primary cortex (Kemmerer and González Castillo 12). Specifically, "outstretched" and "spread" indicate how to position these parts of the body for perfect gripping, and these types of specifications could potentiate its modeling, because when readers process changes in a character's interactions with an object, neurons from brain regions associated with grasping hand movements resonate intensely (Speer et al. 996).

After sequencing the specky, the narrator offers some background to its success:

> Specky practised his high marking by kicking the ball onto the roof of his house, and then timing his run to jump at exactly the split second the ball came bouncing down off the tiles and spilling over the guttering. It improved his marking dramatically [...]. (7)

"Kicking" is a well-researched verb in studies of motor imagery, and it has been shown that subjects who mentally rehearse place-kicking improve their kicking abilities (Moran 132) – although place-kicking has not been used in Rules for over half a century. More generally, as Ross-Stewart notes, performance is enhanced in the long term by repeating the process of imagining accurate motor execution and control sequences (39). Adding meticulous information about timing, as implied by the phrase "at exactly the split second," is crucial for the potential of a motor resonance to correlate with better practice (Moran 130–134). Additionally, vividness is a key feature of mental imagery to improve sport ability (Moran 120), and the description certainly captures this Rules movement with exactitude.

Even though the sequence of movements required to perform a specky and the other techniques required in Rules are specified in detail throughout the novel, they remain challenging football moves. Moreover, while it is true that reading about physical movements activates the motor system, we do not yet know what the specific behavioral effects of that activation are. This remains problematic to predict particularly for overweight cohorts, whose performance and motivation may be quite compromised. I would suggest that the potential of motor resonances to increase exercise motivation in response to Specky's physical performance is subject to overweight readers being impacted by the narrative.

Narrative Impact in *Specky Magee*

Reader engagement with *Specky Magee* is achieved because, technically, Specky is the text's only focalizer, and he is beset with a problem likely to make readers inclined to sympathize. In particular, the protagonist suspects that he is adopted since he found a photograph of himself as a baby dressed in football gear, but his family dislikes this sport and they are unsupportive of Specky's love for it. Acknowledging the inevitable variation that would exist amongst real readers' responses, as well as the cognitive specificities of children's reading (Nikolajeva 19), I suggest that there are three specific narrative features of *Specky Magee* with the ability to impact readers and prompt them to do sport. In the first place, the positive affectivity sparked by the protagonist's successful football movements has the potential to generate cognitive reappraisals of physical activity. Cognitive reappraisal consists in the reinterpretation of the meaning of a situation to modify its emotional valence, for example to lower aversive thoughts generated by it. The passage where the narrator finishes the description of the specky sequence could lead to cognitive reappraisal in readers initially unwilling to exercise:

With a confident grip on the ball, the mark was taken directly in front of the big sticks. Specky landed on the ground with a thud and grinned to himself as he heard the umpire's whistle sound the end of the game. Specky was allowed to take his kick for goal. (7)

Lack of self-confidence is one of the reasons why overweight children specifically are less eager to engage in physical activity (Fiorilli et al. 38). Characterizing the grip of the ball as "confident" prevents the arousal of this emotion, and in fact encourages the interpretation that modeling this movement is feasible. In reluctant overweight exercisers, perceived behavioral control is generally predictive of engagement in the context of exercising (Fiorilli et al. 43).

Information about smiling at the end of the specky sequence also directs readers' attention to Specky's emotional state as he lands. Succeeding in sports is not restricted to winning contests; it is also related with positive affective reactions generated by physical activity. Ekkekakis and Zenko emphasize the relevance of positive affective conditionings of past experiences with physical activity to increase motivation to exercise (406). For overweight children, as a result of diminished cardiovascular endurance, any form of physical activity can be associated with aversive thoughts (Fiorilli et al. 38). The phrase "grinned to himself" reappraises the act of jumping. It codifies this leap as a positive motor experience, potentially increasing readers' motivation to try it.

Even though the protagonist's specky is a successful one, the kicking of the ball afterwards does not result in him scoring a goal. Specky's attention is diverted, causing him to kick off-target. The protagonist's distraction is explained by the fact that a rival mentions the absence of Specky's father at the match. Specky feels his passion for Rules is disregarded since, while other fathers frequently attend the game to see their sons play, Specky's never does. The scene consequently acquires a touching tone.

The second way in which *Specky Magee* is likely to impact children is, then, through empathizing with the protagonist. The result of Specky's distraction greatly embarrasses him, and his resulting mood of shame would arguably trigger a feeling of empathy in readers (Oatley 106). An experience of empathy increases the likelihood that a narrative will lead to persuasive outcomes (Shen 400), as well as to undergo stronger motor imagery activation (Wilson et al. 419). Moreover, readers are less likely to be impacted by a narrative if dealt with unrealistically (Lu 3). Hence, missing a score adds veracity to the protagonist's skills and persuasive potential to the scene.

During the next match, the protagonist redeems his failed shot, performing a perfect specky, which encourages the team to play well for the rest of the game. The narrator establishes an opposition between the henceforth cheating rivals and the dexterity with which Specky avoids them:

> They tried to trip, punch and injure Specky in any way they could. But Specky was too nimble and agile for them all. He ducked, twisted and turned, avoiding all their dirty tactics. (18)

The dirty tactics of these opponents may prompt readers to experience pride and empathy for the protagonist, and thus perhaps to feel motivated to emulate his agile maneuvers. Furthermore, this contrast with Specky's physical grace breaks the motif of masculine power and aggression as essential to Australian sporting culture (McAdams 249). Romøren and Stephens coined the term "metonymic configuration" (223) to refer to these gender challenges in Australian sports literature, and this technique is employed repeatedly by Arena and Lyon.

The pressure of sporting competitiveness reduces the motivation of overweight children to engage in sports (Fiorilli et al. 43). It is consistent practice that has allowed Specky to become so agile, and the narrator offers an example of training away from the field likely to produce another cognitive reappraisal of physical activity. In particular, Specky engages in a "friendly" kicking game with a girl called Christina. The characterization of kicking as "friendly" deprives this action of competitiveness, enabling readers' appraisal of kicking as a positive affective experience. This is reinforced through the reference to the space used for practice: the backyard provides a sense of calmness contrasting with the typical fictionalized setting of the football field (Hogan 135). It is advisable for overweight youngsters who are reluctant to exercise to feel at ease with their surroundings when doing exercise, because this contributes to enhancing their self-efficacy (Fiorilli et al. 43). After finishing, both characters smile, further facilitating a positive mental reenactment of the scene.

On the subject of reenactment, the simulation hypothesis (Oatley 101) has been formulated to account for the occasions when readers simulate characters' experiences in narratives. This is the final way in which I suggest that the novel may impact readers and persuade them to exercise. According to this hypothesis, simulating the events that happen to a character increases the understanding of what it is like to experience them, and beliefs may be consequently influenced.

Simulation is claimed to occur when readers experience a story from the viewpoint of a given character, and this dovetails with the capacity of a narrative to impact readers, particularly through character–reader similarity. Similarity can be based on objective or subjective characteristics. According to De Graaf, relatedness in objective characteristics, like age or sex, increases the likelihood that a reader will be persuaded on subjective matters, like healthy attitudes or habits (74). Owing to the fact that *Specky Magee* is targeted at children between 9 and 13, many could feel related to Specky, a 12-year-old, and follow his passion for football. Furthermore, the popularity of the series in Australia has been well confirmed. In 2008, it placed at number three in the poll conducted by Angus and Robertson, ranking higher than any other Australian author ever in the Kids' Top 5 (*Sunshine Coast Daily* par. 3), which attests to the scope of its influence.

For overweight readers, there is one reference to a character in the story which could especially facilitate the experience of simulation. In particular, the novel includes a description about a heavy character able to beat Specky:

> He was forced to play opposite Mrs Kavensky, the sausage sizzle lady and a former Olympian shot-putter who weighed over 100 kg. Specky was slaughtered by her, especially when she executed a "hip and shoulder"! (19)

This passage is noteworthy, as it focuses on a sportswoman who is probably overweight (we do not know her height), an Olympic champion and a football player – an unfamiliar combination, although the fictional presence of women in Rules can be traced to the nineteenth century (Hutchinson 18). According to De Graaf, observed similarity determines self-perceived efficacy (85). Since readers can identify with the fact that she was able to "slaughter" the protagonist, simulating Kavensky may be effective to persuade overweight readers to play more confidently. This brings the discussion to the health-giving and persuasive effects of narratives, and to the influence wielded by stories on readers' physical activity motivation.

The Inspiring Value of Sports Narratives

Evidence from health communication studies supports the view that narratives focusing on relatable physical activity exert a positive impact on readers' attitudes and behaviors toward exercising. In one of the earliest health communication experiments on exercise behaviors,

Rimer and Glassman discovered that participants in the experimental group, who were provided with an exercise booklet, engaged in more physical activity when they related the information to their own lives than when they did not (313). In more recent investigations, Lu, for example, measured participants' intention to engage in running, finding that it was stronger after reading entry blogs in a personalized narrative condition than in the nonnarrative one. In her pilot and follow-up experiment, Boeijinga found that tailoring a fictional narrative to the "intention to exercise" stage caused truck drivers to improve their determination to exercise (101).

With regard to sociological data about the relationship between sports media and exercising, the 2017 Aussie-FIT pilot study engaged 130 overweight Australian football fans to investigate whether their passion could be useful in a health intervention. The project was successful, helping the fans to lose weight and adopt a healthier lifestyle (5–7). Furthermore, there are certain investigations which offer correlative results between reading and exercise habits – although not causal relationships. For instance, Wilson provided evidence from a sample of US children that higher frequency of reading sports books correlated with higher exercising rates (27–51). Spreitzer and Snyder reported evidence from a US sample that black communities were both further engaged in reading sports books and exercising than white subjects (56).

These investigations, nonetheless, do not clarify the specific processes that readers undergo during exposure that improve their physical activity attitudes and habits. There is an established body of evidence showing that engaging in motor imagery activities encourages athletes and non-athletes to exercise. This could be an explanation for the findings of these studies. Ross-Stewart surveyed the available empirical evidence about sportspeople, concluding that motor imagery is used by athletes to increase their motivation and exercise more (30–31). Additionally, she gathered evidence about the effect of an experimental manipulation using a motor imagery script with instructions on a sample of non-exercising subjects. In one group, subjects were asked to imagine themselves engaged in physical activity. In the other group, participants were provided with an exercise informational brochure and no explicit instructions. Results revealed that exercise frequency level increased significantly in both conditions, although more so in the brochure condition (67). Sherman et al. also reported evidence from a sample of non-exercising subjects. They showed that participants increased their exercise frequency in the week after watching a video about physical activity while imagining themselves copying the exercises (461).

Investigations of the effects of reading books specifically on motor imagery are lacking, although some experiments have been conducted to research the neurological effects of reading. In one study, Speer et al. reported fMRI evidence that reading passages from *One Boy's Day* (1951), an observational account which included descriptions of how the subject, Raymond, "walked briskly" or "hurried back to his desk," provoked 28 participants to use motor representations to follow the story (997). Additionally, Berns et al. provided fMRI evidence from a sample of 21 participants, who were offered Harris's *Pompeii* (2003) to read, that long-term changes in connectivity were observed in their somatosensory cortices after reading (598). Hartung and Willems also offered fMRI data from a sample of 57 subjects whose supplementary motor areas were activated while reading action and movement scenes in two short stories (47). Finally, in an experimental study carried out by Natalie Phillips and researchers at the Stanford Center for Cognitive and Neurobiological Imaging, it was found that participants who read a chapter from Jane Austen's *Mansfield Park* (1814) had their motor cortex area strongly activated. Phillips concluded that these were brain activation patterns of "a region dedicated to the physical control and mental imagery of movement" (219).

Researchers in all these cases claim that their experiments provide evidence in support of embodied simulation in the context of narrative reading. These results endorse the idea that stories focusing on action and movement changes trigger motor resonances in readers. Although speculatively, I suggest using the findings hitherto gathered as a source of evidence to defend the hypothesis that reading a sports novel could increase participants' commitment to physical activity. In a nutshell, characters' sports experiences would habituate readers to run covert mental simulations of physical activity, making more likely their actual engagement in physical activity due to increases in experienced motivation to move.

There may be specific benefits of reading novels to support a health intervention of this kind. Marsh and colleagues provided experimental evidence about a phenomenon provoked by reading stories called the "absolute sleeper effect," where the persuasive effects of a narrative remain after it has been finished. They found that participants' beliefs about nine experimental textoids were maintained after one week of reading (533). Experimental textoids are not sufficiently ecologically valid, however: published fiction differs from texts created specifically for laboratory testing. Appel and Richter replicated Marsh's findings in a similar experiment but using two published short stories, and found strong endorsement of beliefs after two weeks (125). This kind of persistence in the effects of narrative reading could be an effective mechanism in health interventions, although their impact may still be decreased by the relative shortness of these texts. Due to its increased length, a novel like *Specky Magee* could have a long-term effect, further increasing the persuasive impact on readers to persevere in remaining physically active, because changes in brain connectivity persist over time after closing a book (Berns et al. 591).

Reclaiming a therapeutic role from a novel in this manner might be suspect of reifying the "translational imperative" of neuroscience, which "demands that research be applicable in the form of products and therapies" (Vidal and Ortega 77). Certainly, this chapter has added a pragmatic dimension to the analysis of *Specky Magee*. The purpose has been a health-giving one: employing this story to aid Australian children to engage in physical activity. Regardless, complementing literary analysis with neuroscientific evidence to seek an extrinsic function for fiction does not deprive it of its intrinsic value. As regards sports fiction, the positive references one might argue about its inherent worth are notable, since it transmits deep morals about the value of peer cooperation and support from friends and family. As Specky's father eventually realizes that he must partake in his son's passion for Rules, these are values well represented in *Specky Magee*.

Conclusion: Fitness in Fiction

Fiction, according to literary Darwinism, creates opportunities for adaptive processes to unfold (Nikolajeva 76). There might be no greater argument for supporting the value of fiction than to show that it is essential to our fitness. Admittedly, this notion of fitness differs from the physical connotation of the word in the sports field, and yet the basic idea holds true for both viewpoints: fiction provides readers with selective advantages through the grounded simulation of scenarios it allows.

To take advantage of embodied modeling in the health persuasion intervention proposed here implies interpreting the actions of fictional characters as experiences of movement that resonate in readers' minds, potentially encouraging them to adopt a physically active lifestyle. Motor resonances are an affordance of sports narratives like *Specky Magee*, with its characteristic emphasis on instructions to perform well at football. Nonetheless, such motor resonances are in need of a narrative engagement on the part of its Australian readership. Overweight children initially hesitant about exercising can tread in Specky's footsteps because his confident dexterity is admirable, and the empathetic link that readers generate with his story is one of the secrets to being motivated to model his actions.

The modeling of characters' actions by readers would be a product of the kind of co-authorship characteristic of Australian sports fiction, exemplified here in the partnership between Lyon and Arena. As an ex-Rules player, Lyon incorporates the embodied nature of football into the story, while Arena tickles the imagination of his usual young targets. Together, they weave the fabric of the dreams of Australian children, opening the door to helping many feel included in football.

Works Cited

Appel, Markus, and Tobias Richter. "Persuasive Effects of Fictional Narratives Increase Over Time." *Media Psychology*, vol. 10, no. 1, 2007, pp. 113–134.

Aussie-FIT. "Findings from the Aussie-FIT Pilot Study." *Aussiefit*, 2019. http://www.aussiefit.org/uploads/9/7/3/6/9736343/aussie-fit_pilot_project_-_summary_brochure.pdf.

Australian Bureau of Statistics. "National Health Survey." *ABS*, June 19, 2019. https://www1.health.gov.au/internet/main/publishing.nsf/Content/Overweight-and-Obesity.

Berns, Gregory S., Kristina Blaine, Michael J. Prietula, and Brandon E. Pye. "Short- and Long-Term Effects of a Novel on Connectivity in the Brain." *Brain Connectivity*, vol. 3, no. 6, 2013, pp. 590–600.

Boeijinga, Anniek. *Story Bridging: A Narrative Approach to Health Promotion for Dutch Truck Drivers*. Colophon, 2018.

De Graaf, Anneke. "The Effectiveness of Adaptation of the Protagonist in Narrative Impact: Similarity Influences Health Beliefs Through Self-Referencing." *HCR*, vol. 40, 2014, pp. 73–90.

Ekkekakis, Panteleimon, and Zachary, Zenko. "Escape from Cognitivism: Exercise as Hedonic Experience." *Sport and Exercise Psychology Research: From Theory to Practice*, edited by Markus Raab, Paul Wylleman, Roland Seiler, Anne-Marie Elbe, and Antonis Hatzigeorgiadis. Academic Press, 2016, pp. 389–414.

Fiorilli, Giovanni, Enzo, Iuliano, Giovanna, Aquino, Emidio, Campanella, Despina, Tsopani, Alfonso, Di Costanzo, Giuseppe, Calcagno, and Alessandra di Cagno. "Different Consecutive Training Protocols to Design an Intervention Program for Overweight Youth: A Controlled Study." *Dovepress*, vol. 10, 2017, pp. 37–45.

Foster, John. "Popular Fiction for the Cyber-generation." *Bush, City, Cyberspace: The Development of Australian Children's Literature into the 21st Century*, edited by John Foster, Ern Finnis, and Maureen Nimon. Elsevier, 2005, pp. 117–130.

Fuelscher, Ian, Karen, Caeyenberghs, Peter Gregory, Enticott, Melissa, Kirkovski, Shawna, Farquharson, Jarrad, Lum, and Hyde Christian. "Does fMRI Repetition Suppression Reveal Mirror Neuron Activity in the Human Brain? Insights from Univariate and Multivariate Analysis." *EJN*, vol. 50, 2019, pp. 2877–2892.

2008 "Harry Potter's King." *Sunshine Coast Daily*, 19 March 2008, https:// www.sunshinecoastdaily.com.au/news/harry-potters-king/336464/.

Hartung, Franziska, and Roel M. Willems. "Amount of Fiction Reading Correlates with Higher Connectivity Between Cortical Areas for Language and Mentalizing." *bioRxiv*, 2020, pp. 1–69.

Hogan, Tim. *Reading the Game: An Annotated Guide to the Literature and Films of Australian Rules Football*. Australian Society for Sports History, 2005.

Hutchinson, Garrie. *The Great Australian Book of Football Stories*. Currey O'Neil, 1983.

Kemmerer, David, and Javier González Castillo. "The Two-level Theory of Verb Meaning: An Approach to Integrating the Semantics of Action with the Mirror Neuron System." *Brain and Language*, vol. 112, no. 1, 2010, pp. 54–76.

Lu, Amy S. "An Experimental Test of the Persuasive Effect of Source Similarity In Narrative and Nonnarrative Health Blogs." *JMIR*, vol. 15, no. 7, 2013.

Lyon, Garry, and Felice Arena. *Specky Magee*. Penguin Group Australia, 2002.

McAdams, Rachel. *Siren: A Novel and Exegesis Exploring Sexual Violence in Australian Rules Football*. Unpublished PhD diss. Victoria University, 2016.

Moran, Aidan P. *Sport and Exercise Psychology. A Critical Introduction*. Routledge, 2012.

Nikolajeva, Maria. *Reading for Learning: Cognitive Approaches to Children's Literature*. John Benjamins, 2014.

Oatley, Keith. "Why Fiction May Be Twice as True as Fact: Fiction as Cognitive and Emotional Simulation." *Review of General Psychology*, vol. 3, no. 2, 1999, pp. 101–117.

Phillips, Natalie M. "History of Mind and Literary Neuroscience." *Distraction: Problems of Attention in Eighteenth-Century Literature*. John Hopkins, 2016, pp. 212–231.

Romøren, Rolf, and John Stephens. "Representing Masculinity in Young Adult Fiction: A Comparative Study of Examples from Norway and Australia." *Ways of Being Male: Representing Masculinity in Children's Literature and Film*, edited by John Stephens. Routledge, 2002, pp. 216–233.

Ross-Stewart, Lindsay. *The Effect of a One Time Imagery Intervention on Self-Efficacy and Exercise Frequency in a Non-Exercising Population*. Unpublished PhD diss. University of North Dakota, 2009.

Shen, Lijiang. "Mitigating Psychological Reactance: The Role of Message-Induced Empathy in Persuasion." *HCR*, vol. 36, 2010, pp. 397–422.

Sherman, David K., Cynthia, Gangi, and Marina L. White. "Embodied Cognition and Health Persuasion: Facilitating Intention–Behavior." *JESP*, vol. 46, no. 2, 2010, pp. 461–464.

Speer, Nicole K., Jeremy R. Reynolds, Khena M. Swallow, and Jeffrey M. Zacks. "Reading Stories Activates Neural Representations of Visual and Motor Experiences." *Psychological Science*, vol. 20, no. 8, 2009, pp. 989–999.

Spreitzer, Elmer, and Eldon E. Snyder. "Sports Within the Black Subculture: A Matter of Social Class or a Distinctive Subculture?" *JSSI*, vol. 14, no. 1, 1990, pp. 48–58.

Vidal, Fernando, and Francisco Ortega. *Being Brains: Making the Cerebral Subject.* Fordham, 2017.

Wilson, Christine, Dave, Smith, Paul, Holmes, and Adrian Burden. "Participant-generated Imagery Scripts Produce Greater EMG Activity and Imagery Ability." *European Journal of Sport Science*, vol. 10, no. 6, 2010, pp. 417–425.

Wilson, Wayne. "Children and Sports Media." Amateur Athletic Foundation of Los Angeles, 1999.

8 Feeling the Land: Embodied Relations in Contemporary Aboriginal Fiction

Dorothee Klein

Introduction

Aboriginal writing frequently draws attention to the significance of being interrelated with the land, or Country, in terms of a bodily interconnectedness, and thus foregrounds an inextricable link between body, mind, and environment – a link that is also central to the second-generation cognitive sciences.[1] In this chapter, I draw on recent approaches to embodiment to explore the various ways in which contemporary Aboriginal narratives convey a notion of feeling the land through embodied simulation. By employing different textual markers to evoke bodily reactions, these works give form to an understanding of the land where the boundary between the body and the physical world dissolves. Several recent studies show how insights from cognitive science allow for a better understanding of the diverse forms of environmental imagination that narratives mediate, debate, and construct (e.g. James; Weik von Mossner). A close analysis of textual strategies through the lens of 4E cognition helps to explain how reading can constitute what Erin James, in her cognitive ecocritical analysis of postcolonial narratives, terms "a virtual form of environmental experience" (xi). By attending to the literary forms used to "encode environmental meaning" (James 29), I seek to show how Aboriginal fiction implicates the reader's body to convey the vitality of the land and to potentially elicit moments of corporeal interconnectedness.[2]

In the following, I will first provide a brief outline of the significance of embodiment for the comprehension of narrative. I then explore the poetics and politics of embodied relations in Aboriginal fiction based on two sets of examples that elucidate different textual strategies for prompting a sense of embodied participation. While Scott's *Benang* (1999) and Alexis Wright's *Carpentaria* (2006) allude to visceral functions such as breathing and heartbeats, my other two examples, Scott's *Taboo* (2017) and Tara June Winch's *The Yield* (2019), address the embodied dimension of local languages. The final part explicates how Aboriginal fiction, through its emphasis on feeling the land, engages with recent discourses on humanity's relationship with the natural environment by foregrounding the need to recognize our interconnectedness.

The Significance of Embodiment

In *Story About Feeling*, a collection of oral narratives, the late Gagudju elder "Big" Bill Neidjie uses an "embodied form of teaching" and stresses "intercorporeality" (Morrissey 3; 2) to introduce non-Aboriginal readers to Aboriginal knowledge. Understanding the land through storytelling, Neidjie shows, cannot happen independently of the body:

> This story e coming through you body,
> e go right down foot and head, fingernail and blood...
> through the heart. (19)

Here, the story literally travels through the body. Overall, Neidjie presents storytelling as well as listening to stories as a decidedly embodied activity that is rooted in the local land.

Aboriginal oral stories such as Neidjie's *Story About Feeling* exhibit an understanding of the central role of the body that has only recently become a cornerstone of cognitive science and which contradicts the long-held conviction in Western thought that the human mind is self-contained and separated from the body and the physical world. These so-called 4E, or "second-generation" approaches, diverge from earlier conceptualizations of the mind as an abstract entity by foregrounding its embodied, embedded, enactive, and extended qualities. As Mark Rowlands explains, *embodied* means that cognitive processes are part of bodily structures; they are *embedded* in the broader physical and cultural environment; they are *enacted* because they depend on corporeal activities rather than just neural processes; and they are *extended* since they reach into the material environment (3).

From the perspective of 4E cognition, bodily experiences are essential for our engagement with and interpretation of literary texts, as empirical work shows, for instance on embodied simulation in language comprehension (e.g., Bergen) and the reading process (e.g.,

Gallese and Wojciehowski). According to the embodied simulation hypothesis, when we read a sentence we mentally simulate the actions that are being described (Bergen 13). These simulations are not always conscious, but frequently occur beneath the surface (Bergen 14). Reading, then, as Karin Kukkonen explains, "depends on embodied resonances of the motion verbs, descriptions of bodily states, and directions in the written language" (4). Attending to the embodied dimension of language therefore helps to elucidate how the body is implicated in our reading of literary texts, for instance through textual markers that trigger certain bodily reactions or that bring embodied simulations of actions and perceptions to the level of conscious reflection.

This focus on embodiment is a promising avenue to integrate cognitive insights into cultural studies – a project that is still in its infancy (e.g., Hartner; Zunshine). Conceiving of narratives as situated or embedded in specific contexts, cognitive literary studies in the wake of second-generation cognitive science aim to bring cognitive and cultural aspects to bear on each other. If the body constitutes "a 'site of conversion' between physical patterns of interaction with the world and cultural, linguistic meanings," as Kukkonen and Caracciolo argue (267–268), then attending to the dimension of embodied language in the mediation of environmental experiences opens up a window into diverse ways of understanding our relationship with the physical world and different cultural meanings attached to it. This is not to suggest that Aboriginal fiction can be regarded as a transparent reflection or quasi-ethnographic account of Indigenous onto-epistemologies. Instead, such a reading probes the potential of narrative to encourage a rethinking of our relation to the natural environment by translating culture-specific conceptualizations and imaginings of the environment into basic embodied experiences.

In "Sovereign Bodies of Feeling," Alison Ravenscroft describes how, during her travels with two Aboriginal women, she came to ask herself to what extent the fact that she is an embodied subject enculturated in a specific environment has an impact on the kind of relationship she has with the country. She proposes that different perceptions of the environment, and the ability to "make sense" of the land in the meaning of "to sense it, feel it" (1), have to do with the degree to which the "sensate body" (1) is "attuned" to the vitality of the land "as a result of cultural practices" (6). Aboriginal narratives do not necessarily teach us what it means to look at the land through "Aboriginal eyes," but through their implication of basic human visceral functions, such as breathing and heartbeats, they build a bridge to cross cultural divides. My focus in this chapter is accordingly primarily on simulation, as triggered by textual cues, rather than interpretation in the sense of attaching cultural meanings to these embodied experiences.

With their distinct focus on embodied relations with the natural environment, Aboriginal fictional narratives therefore provide particularly fertile case studies to test the advantages of bringing Australian literature into dialog with cognitive (literary) studies. As I will demonstrate, these narratives suggest that the environment plays an essential role in cognitive processes and thus address a central question currently debated in research on 4E cognition, namely in what ways cognition involves extracranial processes. At the same time, reading these novels through the lens of 4E cognition provides insights into the possibilities of narrative to mediate locally specific environmental experiences through embodied simulations, thereby generating a reading that negotiates human commonality and cultural particularity.

Embodied Simulation in Kim Scott's *Benang* and Alexis Wright's *Carpentaria*

Scott's *Benang* and Wright's *Carpentaria* both employ highly embodied language that refers to visceral activities to convey the vitality of the land. In *Benang*, this is primarily achieved through the mediation and evocation of heartbeats and breathing. One chapter, for example, tellingly titled "*blooms its heartbeat*," ends on the following note: "The mist hangs above the rocks where the big sea blooms. Blooms. Booms. Booms its heartbeat" (469). Visual perception here turns into an auditory and ultimately visceral experience. The fragmented syntax and monosyllabic words with long vowel sounds slow down the narrative speed and introduce a specific rhythm, including breaks, which resonates with the reader's own heartbeat. The onomatopoeic "booms" furthermore imitates the sound of a beating heart. The highly rhythmic quality of this passage thereby prompts an embodied simulation of a regular heartbeat. The sea is compared to our own visceral system and associated with the human heart that constantly pumps blood through our body and thus guarantees life.

Rhythmic syntax may also suggest a specific breathing pattern to trigger a simulation of environmental vitality and corporeal interconnectedness. Hovering above the campfire, Harley, who has a tendency to float in the air, looks down on the coastline and feels its breath:

> The sea, like the fire, formed and reformed and out by the island – even at night – there was that blossoming; white, gone, white, gone white gone. Like what? Like ectoplasm, like breathing.
> Here.
> Here.
> Here. (189)

This passage again stages a movement from the visual to the visceral, intimating a need to not only observe but to feel the sea and its particular rhythm. As with the passage above, the starting point is the blossoming of the sea; yet, what follows is not a detailed description that would intensify visualization, but rather an alternating listing of two states: white and gone. Through the punctuation at the beginning of the list, the narrative invites us to adopt a regular rhythm, which we are asked to maintain once the punctuation is left out. The text hence guides us into a rhythmic reading and breathing, which is then explicitly reflected in the subsequent similes. The reference to "ectoplasm," which signifies a transformation of the spirit world into a corporeal presence, suggests that this passage triggers a turn from the unnoticeable to the noticeable. What becomes physically noticeable is our rhythmic breathing, which culminates in three long exhales – "Here. Here. Here" – that associate breathing with spatial situatedness.

The progression in this passage from a simulation of breathing, elicited by monosyllabic words and receding punctuation, to an explicit reflection of that simulation leads us into an embodied understanding of the land, in which storyteller, listener, and place overlap. Harley, as the narrator, translates the rhythm of the sea into words that trigger a rhythmic breathing pattern. The narrative thus creates a moment of synchronicity: Harley feels the land and its breath, and by reading and breathing along, the reader shares in this moment of experiencing the land through the body. In this instance, Harley's fictional body and the reader's actual body are interconnected in a fictional place, "Here." This is a place, amongst others, that deeply affects Harley's narration – as he states later, he "took on the sounds of a place" (384). The narrative makes this place experientially accessible to us by briefly fusing three levels of embodiment: the narrator, the reader, and the sea, who all breathe "Here." As Scott explains, "the narrator's utterances are the sounds of the place in which they are made: bird calls, footfalls, the sound of waves on the beach" ("Covered" 123). There is no boundary between the speaker's body and the natural environment, and by simulating the sea's breath, we can temporarily experience this moment of corporeal inter-connectedness.

More broadly speaking, *Benang* invites us to think of embodied cognition as "*strongly embodied by extrabodily processes*," as one claim in the ongoing debate about the nature of embodiment, and the precise link between brain, body, and environment, puts it (Newen et al. 6). The narrative renders salient the constitutive role of such "extrabodily processes" by foregrounding the extent to which Harley's narration is not only causally dependent on the environment but essentially con-stituted by it. This embodied and embedded form of storytelling ulti-mately functions as a counternarrative to the disembodied stories Harley finds in the "dusty archives" (*Benang* 21) in that it speaks of continuous Aboriginal presence and relation with the land rather than only absence and loss.

Whereas the two passages from *Benang* use rhythmic syntax and play with sound and repetition to elicit an embodied simulation of the vitality of the environment, *Carpentaria* challenges this potential of simulation to enable an embodied understanding of the land. This challenge partly results from the ways in which the novel's evocation of breathing links the notion of feeling the land to the transfer of knowledge and its limits. From the beginning, the novel is deeply in-vested in a form of knowledge that stands in contrast to the one as-sumed by "a nation [who] chants, *but we know your story already*" (1). *Carpentaria* begins with a description of how the ancestral serpent created the region around the Gulf of Carpentaria. Included in this story of ancestral creation, the narrative claims, is "inside knowledge about this river and the coastal region," that is, "the Aboriginal law" (3). This knowledge is an embodied one, because, as the narrator ex-plains, "It takes a particular kind of knowledge to go with the river [...] It is about there being no difference between you and the movement of water" (3). The opening paragraphs include references to breathing in order to convey this relation between bodily feeling and knowledge, or what the Indigenous legal scholar C. F. Black calls "*feeling* of knowledge" (4). This does not mean that *Carpentaria* provides the non-Aboriginal reader with insights into Waanyi onto-epistemologies, as advocated by Frances Devlin-Glass and criticized by Alison Ravenscroft ("Dreaming"). The novel rather cues bodily reactions only to immediately scrutinize the extent to which these embodied simulations help us engage with the vitality of the depicted environment and the knowledge contained in it. As in *Benang*, the narrative moves from a visual to a sensory relationship with the land. While the opening paragraphs ask us to "picture the creative serpent" (1), the subsequent passages draw on breathing as an analogy for the river's movement.

> This tidal river snake of flowing mud takes in breaths of size that is difficult to comprehend. Imagine the serpent's breathing rhythms as the tide flows inland, edging towards the spring waters nestled deeply in the gorges of an ancient limestone plateau covered with rattling grasses dried yellow from the prevailing winds. Then the outward breath, the tide turns and the serpent flows back to its own circulating mass of shallow waters in the giant water basin in a crook of the mainland whose sides separate it from the open sea. (2)

This passage evokes a visceral activity, breathing, through its explicit reference to inhalation and exhalation and the narrative's appeal to "imagine the serpent's breathing rhythms" entails an implicit cue for embodied simulation. According to Marco Caracciolo, imagination entails a simulation or enactment of "a hypothetical perceptual experience" (95). Imagining the serpent's breathing thus cues us to simulate a breathing rhythm, based on our experience of what it is like to take deep, regular breaths.

However, unlike the passage from *Benang* analyzed previously, the text does not contain any specific markers that guide us unequivocally into "the serpent's breathing rhythms." On the one hand, the long, uninterrupted sentences provide a parallel structure in which the first sentence is associated with inhaling – "the tide flows inland" – and the second one with exhaling – "then the outward breath" – and thus resemble a rhythmic, slow breathing. (Indeed, one would have to take a deep breath to read one of these sentences aloud in one breath without speeding up.) On the other hand, a profound question remains: How does a serpent breathe? The narrative does not only make explicit that the size of the serpent's breaths "is difficult to comprehend," but it also makes us aware of the limits of experiencing corporeal interconnectedness through embodied simulation. The narrative alludes to a superimposition of the physical land and the human body by explicitly inviting us to imagine the serpent's breathing and hence implicitly prompts us to simulate it. However, while we may simulate a regular breathing, this is not necessarily a conscious activity (see Kuzmičová, "Literary Narrative" 278–280 on the problem of consciousness). Unlike the passage from *Benang*, the passage from *Carpentaria* neither includes a call for reflection that would pull our embodied simulations to the level of conscious experience, nor does it fuse different levels of embodiment to create a moment of corporeal interconnectedness. It invites us to imagine the inextricable link between the environment that the ancestral serpent created and the people to whom the serpent is "attached […] like skin" (2), but it does not openly guide us into a reading that enacts this notion of feeling the land and the knowledge contained in it.

Embodied Language in Tara June Winch's *The Yield* and Kim Scott's *Taboo*

By drawing on visceral activities such as heartbeats and breathing to simulate an embodied relationship with the land and sea, *Benang* and *Carpentaria* highlight the significance of "having feelings – not emotions, but rather a sensitivity to one's surrounding," as Black has pointed out in the context of Indigenous jurisprudence (17). This sensitivity to the environment is also a central component of Indigenous languages (Scott, "Covered" 123). The revitalization of Indigenous languages, and their growing presence in contemporary writing, constitutes another area in which the interconnectedness of body and land potentially comes to the fore. In Scott's *Taboo* (2017) and Winch's *The Yield* (2019), language, and its embodied, relational dimension, take center stage. Nevertheless, these works do not contain textual features that trigger an embodied simulation of feeling the land, even though, on the level of content, they are deeply invested in the close relation between people, language, and the local land. *The Yield* rather foregrounds the body's role in the production of language through explicit references to actual pronunciation, and *Taboo* sidelines an embodied understanding altogether. They are thus a counterpoint to the examples analyzed previously in that they highlight the limits of sharing diverse (environmental) experiences through embodied simulation. Instead, they scrutinize more the position the (non-Aboriginal) reader occupies.

Drawing on *A New Wiradjuri Dictionary*, compiled by Dr. Stan Grant Sr. and Dr. John Rudder, *The Yield* is partly written in the form of dictionary entries by the protagonist's grandfather, Albert Gondiwindi. His aim is to reclaim a language that is believed to be extinct. From the very beginning, the novel shows that a shift in language forms a shift in perspective: "I was born on *Ngurambang* – can you hear it? – *Ngu-ram-bang*. If you say it right it hits the back of your mouth and you should taste blood in your words" (1). These opening sentences highlight the physicality of language by alluding to the actual pronunciation of the word, and the place of articulation where its first and last sounds are produced, namely the velar region. By directing the reader's attention to the muscular activity of pronouncing the word, the text equates the anatomical place of articulation in the speaker's mouth with the geographical place, Ngurambang, or Australia. Its reference to blood thus becomes more immediate as it implicates our mouth, and its capacity for taste, into the reading of the local land and the place telling titled "Massacre Plains" (13) in the novel. Colonial violence hence does not remain an abstract and disembodied notion, but is directly linked to our physical bodies – and to literally tasting blood.

This direct and explicit implication of our articulatory apparatus becomes even more noticeable in the dictionary entry for "mouth – *ngaan*": "Use the mouth now, say our words aloud," Albert Gondiwindi instructs us, and goes on to explain a variety of sounds found in the Wiradjuri language (155). To convey an impression of those sounds for which there is no equivalent in the English language, he draws comparisons to fundamental visceral activities, such as breathing: "'*nh*' is not heard in English at all – it's like making a breath, sometimes in and sometimes out after an '*n*' sound" (155). Teaching us how to pronounce these words, Albert's story, as contained in the dictionary he writes, "shows us not only how to read Wiradjuri," Ellen van Neerven argues, "but also how to feel and speak and taste it; it decolonises the throat and tongue". In other words, it mediates a triangulation between language, feeling or tasting, and the land, and through this central implication of our articulatory apparatus requires an active engagement with the narrative.

The position that *The Yield* sets out for the non-Aboriginal reader may be further explained with the help of what Anežka Kuzmičová terms "reverberations," which are conscious experiences of verbal auditory imagery – the "sense of hearing the words on a page" – that can be accessed through introspection ("Outer" 111). Proceeding from empirical work in psychology, she distinguishes between two manifestations: "outer reverberations" position us as listeners to speech voiced by a character, whereas "inner reverberations" originate in our own mouth and throat and thus have a kinesthetic quality (111–112). These two forms, she argues, are connected to different meaning-making processes. Whereas outer reverberations link to spontaneous interpretation, inner reverberations obstruct such instantaneous interpretation (127–128).

The passages from *The Yield* analyzed previously constitute an example of inner reverberations, as they elicit felt motor activity in the vocal tract and thus have a markedly kinesthetic component. However, there are some marked differences to Kuzmičová's theorizing. Whereas she contends that "inner reverberations may be particularly likely to occur with utterances lacking in orality, speaker familiarity and situational embedding" (122), the exact opposite holds for *The Yield*. The passages quoted have a decidedly oral quality, not least due to their use of imperatives and the second-person pronoun to voice a direct address; they exhibit a well-defined speaker, Albert Gondiwindi; and are clearly situated in Wiradjuri Country. What they do show, though, is a high degree of complexity, however not syntactically, as in the examples that Kuzmičová provides (121), but semantically, as aptly captured in the different meanings of the word "yield," "*baayanha*": "yield in English is the reaping, the things that man can take from the land […] In [Wiradjuri] language it's the things you give to, the movement, the space between things" (25). The narrative's focus on pronouncing decidedly situated but semantically opaque speech fundamentally questions one of Kuzmičová's central arguments: "when the voice is mine, then the thought is mine as well. It is only when the voice is not mine that I am left to wonder what the underlying thought and meaning might be" (128). *The Yield* emphasizes that even when the voice is mine, the meaning and the thoughts are not, as they still belong to Albert Gondiwindi and the Wiradjuri language to which he introduces us. The narrative literally teaches us to use our body, especially our articulatory apparatus, to engage with a "language that is connected to this place, this landscape" (Winch 146) as a means to reshape our perception of Australia as Ngurambang. However, as the focus is on the techniques of pronunciation rather than bodily feelings, it foregrounds the need for respect as a prerequisite for crossing cultural divides through embodied simulation.

Ultimately, considering the position that the narrative sets out for non-Wiradjuri readers from the perspective of 4E cognition sheds light on the decolonial imperative of Winch's novel. If reading entails an embodied simulation of the actions and states being described (Bergen 13; Kukkonen 4), then *The Yield* poses an explicit challenge to non-Wiradjuri readers by fundamentally thwarting this process. Its focus on articulation and, at least partial, obstruction of semantic understanding through embodied simulation forces us into the position of a "welcomed stranger" (Wright, "On Writing" 87), since we are reliant on the narrative as a teacher and translator. The novel challenges the settler colonial order and replicates this feeling of unsettlement by exposing us to a language that makes us aware of our own positionality. As the narrative poignantly reminds us, "we forget we're all in someone else's country. And too often we don't have the vision, the respect to bother learning the native language! To even learn to respect the culture where we live?" (299).

This need for a respectful stance toward Aboriginal languages and cultures is also reinforced in Scott's *Taboo*, which takes the opposite approach to *The Yield*. While *Taboo* is also a novel that is deeply informed by language, the Noongar language, it does not include any direct representations thereof. Instead, Scott uses phrases like "in the old language" (e.g., 15, 49, 50, 98, 268) or "the old people's tongue" (e.g., 15, 16) to indicate that the characters switch to Noongar. The reading experience thus generated is one that proceeds from "outer reverberations," positioning us primarily as vicarious listeners. The embodied dimension of language, and its link to the environment, is frequently alluded to but remains more opaque, as in the following passage, when Wilfred, an elder, passes around some wooden artefacts: "He told them the names in the old tongue, and the words started coming to life with their tongue and their mouths and their breath as they handled that timber" (103). Compared to the passages from *The Yield*, the text contains fewer specific anchors for the reader to relate to the embodied dimension of the Noongar language, as it merely refers generally to the physiological basis of all articulation.

Nevertheless, the narrative frequently highlights the interconnectedness between body and land, even though it only renders it in translation: "The word for river in the old language was nearly the same as the word for navel. He [Gerry] liked that; it told you about connection. Words hold everything together" (254). Unlike *The Yield*, *Taboo* does not introduce us to Noongar language as such, but it still draws attention to the link between body and land – a link that we can follow tentatively and vicariously, for instance, by drawing on actual or mediated experiences of bodily connections through the umbilical cord as a life-providing tie. More broadly speaking, *The Yield* foregrounds the embodied dimension of language by physically implicating our articulatory apparatus only to make a clear distinction between pronouncing a language connected to the land and feeling the land. *Taboo*, in contrast, forecloses any explicit embodied simulation. As a reader, feeling the land that "was a massacre place" (3) is literally a taboo.

Conclusion: From Feeling to Caring

In this chapter, I outlined several narrative strategies that encourage a shift in perception toward an intercorporeal understanding of the land as a living organism. My examples can be situated on a continuum, from openly and directly facilitating embodied simulation of environmental vitality, as in *Benang*, to merely addressing the issue thematically, but without any textual cues that would allow for an approach based on bodily feeling, as in *Taboo*. Overall, my analysis of these four novels points out the possibilities and limits of embodied simulation to cross cultural divides, for example regarding different views about the land. On the one hand, they evoke bodily experiences to produce vicarious moments of feeling the land that the reader can engage with through the body without immediately having to attach cultural meanings to these experiences. On the other hand, they may also obstruct this possibility to foreground that what is needed first is a respectful attitude toward Aboriginal cultures.

With this focus on the possibility of feeling the land, these works are arguably, inter alia, a timely intervention into current discourses about humanity's relationship with the environment. By foregrounding bodily feelings, they convey a need for an ethics of caring, as the Tanganekald, Meintangk-Bunganditj legal scholar Irene Watson explains: "Aboriginal caring for the land is equivalent to caring for one's own body; it is an act of self-preservation and self-protection and it engages a deep knowledge of our interdependency" (41). By attending to and exposing the role of the reader's body in processing literary narratives that openly or covertly address the significance of a corporeal interrelatedness with the land, contemporary Aboriginal fiction holds up a mirror to our own understanding of and relationship with the natural environment. Ultimately, these narratives encourage a shift in perspective: away from the land as a material resource toward a view of nature as a vital, living relation.

Notes

1 I am grateful to Sibylle Baumbach for her helpful comments on an earlier version of this chapter.
2 The reader's body that I refer to in this chapter is not gendered. It does, however, belong to a white person, as I cannot speak for Aboriginal readers. Moreover, I am particularly interested in the question of how embodied simulation may function as a bridge to cross cultural divides by foregrounding basic bodily activities such as breathing.

Works Cited

Bergen, Benjamin K. *Louder Than Words: The New Science of How the Mind Makes Meaning*. Basic Books, 2012.

Black, C. F. *The Land Is the Source of the Law: A Dialogic Encounter with Indigenous Jurisprudence*. Routledge, 2011.

Caracciolo, Marco. *The Experientiality of Narrative: An Enactivist Approach*. De Gruyter, 2014.

Devlin-Glass, Frances. "A Politics of the Dreamtime: Destructive and Regenerative Rainbows in Alexis Wright's *Carpentaria*." *Australian Literary Studies*, vol. 23, no. 4, 2008, pp. 392–407.

Gallese, Vittorio, and Hannah Wojciehowski. "How Stories Make Us Feel: Toward an Embodied Narratology." *California Italian Studies*, vol. 2, no. 1, 2011.

Hartner, Marcus. "Bodies, Spaces, and Cultural Models: On Bridging the Gap between Culture and Cognition." *JLT*, vol. 11, no. 2, 2017, pp. 204–222.

James, Erin. *The Storyworld Accord: Econarratology and Postcolonial Narratives*. U of Nebraska P, 2015.

Kukkonen, Karin. *4E Cognition and Eighteenth-Century Fiction: How the Novel Found Its Feet*. Oxford UP, 2019.

Kukkonen, Karin, and Marco Caracciolo. "Introduction: What Is the 'Second Generation'?" *Style*, vol. 48, no. 3, 2014, pp. 261–274.

Kuzmičová, Anežka. "Outer vs. Inner Reverberations: Verbal Auditory Imagery and Meaning-Making in Literary Narrative." *JLT*, vol. 7, no. 1-2, 2013, pp. 111–134.

Kuzmičová, Anežka. "Literary Narrative and Mental Imagery: A View from Embodied Cognition." *Style*, vol. 48, no. 3, 2014, pp. 275–293.

Morrissey, Philip. "Bill Neidjie's *Story About Feeling*: Notes on Its Themes and Philosophy." *JASAL*, vol. 15, no. 2, 2015, pp. 1–11.

Neidjie, Bill. *Story About Feeling*, edited by Keith Taylor, Magabala Books, 1989.

Newen, Albert, et al. "4E Cognition: Historical Roots, Key Concepts, and Central Issues." *The Oxford Handbook of 4E Cognition*, edited by Albert Newen et al., Oxford UP, 2018, pp. 3–15.

Ravenscroft, Alison. "Dreaming of Others: *Carpentaria* and Its Critics." *Cultural Studies Review*, vol. 16, no. 2, 2010, pp. 194–224.

Ravenscroft, Alison. "Sovereign Bodies of Feeling: 'Making Sense' of Country." *JASAL*, vol. 14, no. 3, 2014, pp. 1–9.

Rowlands, Mark. *The New Science of the Mind: From Extended Mind to Embodied Phenomenology*. MIT P, 2010.

Scott, Kim. *Benang: From the Heart*. Fremantle P, 1999.

Scott, Kim. "Covered Up with Sand." *Meanjin Quarterly*, vol. 66, no. 2, 2007, pp. 120–124.

Scott, Kim. *Taboo*. Picador, 2017.

Van Neerven, Ellen. Rev. of *The Yield,* by Tara June Winch. *Australian Book Review*, vol. 413, August 2019, https://www.australianbookreview.com.au/abr-online/archive/2019/author/5025-ellenvanneerven. Accessed 29 May 2020.

Watson, Irene. "Sovereign Spaces, Caring for Country, and the Homeless Position of Aboriginal Peoples." *South Atlantic Quarterly*, vol. 108, no. 1, 2009, pp. 27–51.

Weik von Mossner, Alexa. *Affective Ecologies: Empathy, Emotion, and Environmental Narrative*. Ohio State UP, 2017.

Winch, Tara June. *The Yield*. Hamish Hamilton, 2019.

Wright, Alexis. *Carpentaria*. 2006. Atria Books, 2009.

Wright, Alexis. "On Writing *Carpentaria*." *HEAT*, vol. 13, 2007, pp. 79–95.

Zunshine, Lisa, editor. *Introduction to Cognitive Cultural Studies*. Johns Hopkins UP, 2010.

Cognitive Australian Literary Studies

A Selective Bibliography Compiled by the Editor

Fiction and Nonfiction

Atkinson, Meera Anne. *Traumata*. Queensland UP, 2018.
Bennett, John. "Getting Emotional." *Five Bells*, vol. 10, no. 1, 2002–2003, pp. 13–16.
Black, Katrina. *Distorted Reflections, Misconceptions*. Austed Publishing, 1992, pp. 43–54.
Brooker, Sarah. *My Lucky Stroke*. Affirm Press, 2020.
Bryden, Christine. *Unlocking My Brain: Through the Labyrinth of Acquired Brain Injury*. Ventura Press, 2014.
Carmody, Isobel. *The Obernewtyn Chronicles*. Puffin, 1987.
Caswell, Brian. *Cage of Butterflies*. Queensland UP, 2018.
Durham, Christine. *Doing Up Buttons*. Penguin, 1997.
Egan, Greg. *Quarantine*. Legend, 1992.
Egan, Greg. *Teranesia*. Gollancz, 1999.
Gibbins, Ian. "Lessons in Neuroscience." *Urban Biology*. Wakefield Press/ Friendly Street Poets, 2012, pp. 66–68.
Gibbins, Ian. "Cataplexy." *E Ratio*, vol. 21, 2015, http://www.eratiopost-modernpoetry.com/issue21_Gibbins.html
Gibbins, Ian. "Entorhinal." *Rabbit*, vol. 17, *Geography*, 2016, pp. 60–66.
Gibbins, Ian. "No Glutamate." *Island*, vol. 147, 2016, p. 55.
Jordan, Toni. *Addition*. Text Publishing, 2008.
Lawson, Chris. *Written in Blood*. MirrorDanse Books, 2003.
Lilley, Rozanna. *Do Oysters Get Bored? A Curious Life*. University of Western Australia Publishing, 2018.
McCullough, Colleen. *On, Off*. HarperCollins, 2005.
McFarlane, Fiona. *The Night Guest*. Penguin, 2013.
Meyer, Angela. *A Superior Spectre*. Ventura Press, 2018.
Prendergast, Julia. *The Earth Does Not Get Fat*. University of Western Australia Publishing, 2018.
Prendergast, Julia. "Like Clay," *Double Dialogues*, vol. 19, *The Era of Brokenness*, 2018, http://www.doubledialogues.com/article/like-clay/

Prendergast, Julia. "Much of a Muchness," *TEXT: The Journal of Writing and Writing Courses. Peripheral Visions: Special Issues Series*, vol. 57, 2019, http://www.textjournal.com.au/speciss/issue57/Prendergast.pdf

Redhouse, Nicola. *Unlike the Heart: A Memoir of Brain and Mind.* Queensland UP, 2019.

Robertson, Rachel. *Reaching One Thousand: A Story of Love, Motherhood and Autism*. Black Inc., 2012.

Roland, David. *How I Rescued my Brain*. Scribe, 2014.

Salom, Philip. "The Man Who Mistook His Wife For a Hat." *Feeding the Ghost*. Penguin, 1993, pp. 3–4.

Salom, Philip. "Acupuncturist: Under the Needles," *New and Selected Poems*. Fremantle Arts Centre Press, 1998, pp. 264–266.

Salom, Philip. "Elegy For My Father," *New and Selected Poems*. Fremantle Arts Centre Press, 1998, pp. 258–263.

Salom, Philip. "The Man With a Shattered World," *Alterworld. Puncher & Wattmann*, 2015, pp. 177–181.

Simsion, Graeme. *The Rosie Project*. Text Publishing, 2013.

Simsion, Graeme. *The Rosie Effect*. Text Publishing, 2014.

Simsion, Graeme. *The Rosie Result*. Text Publishing, 2019.

Valentish, Jenny. *Woman of Substances: A Journey into Addiction and Treatment*. Black Inc, 2017.

Vallence, Sarah. *Prognosis: A Memoir of My Brain*. Little A, 2019.

Woolfe, Sue. *The Secret Cure*. Pan MacMillan Australia, 2003.

Simsion, Graeme. *The Mystery of The Cleaning Lady: A Writer Looks at Creativity and Neuroscience*. UWAP, 2007.

Scholarship

Atkinson, Meera Anne. *The Poetics of Transgenerational Trauma.* Bloomsbury, 2017.

Britten, Adrielle. "The Family and Adolescent Wellbeing: Alternative Models of Adolescent Growth in the Novels of Judith Clarke." *International Research in Children's Literature*, vol. 7, no. 2, 2014, pp. 165–179.

Britten, Adrielle. "A Feeling Connection: Embodied Flourishing as Represented in Contemporary Picturebooks." *The Embodied Child: Readings in Children's Literature and Culture*, edited by Roxanne Harde and Lydia Kokkola. Routledge, 2018, pp. 161–174.

Brophy, Kevin. *Patterns of Creativity. Investigations into the Sources and Methods of Creativity*. Rodopi, 2009.

Brophy, Kevin. "The Poet and the Criminal: Dreams, Neuroscience and a Peculiar Way of Thinking," *TEXT*, vol. 18, no. 2, 2014, http://www.textjournal.com.au/oct14/brophy.htm.

Brophy, Kevin, and Sue Woolfe. "Talking about Creativity and Neuroscience." *Island*, vol. 111, 2007, pp. 8–17.

Brydon, Diana. "Experimental Writing and Reading across Borders in Decolonizing Contexts." *ARIEL: A Review of International English Literature*, vol. 47, no. 1-2, 2016, pp. 27–58.

Clarke, Robert. "Intimate Strangers: Contemporary Australian Travel Writing and the Semiotics of Empathy." *Journal of Australian Studies*, vol. 85, 2005, pp. 69–81.

Dalziell, Rosamund. *Shameful Autobiographies: Shame in Contemporary Australian Autobiographies and Culture.* Melbourne UP, 1999.

Denham, Ben. "Difficult Sense: The Neuro-Physical Dimensions of the Act of Reading." *Literature and Sensation*, edited by Anthony Uhlmann, Helen Groth, Paul Sheehan, and Stephen McLaren. Cambridge Scholars Publishing, 2009, pp. 112–121.

Gandolfo, Enza. "Take a Walk in Their Shoes: Empathy and Emotion in the Writing Process." *TEXT: The Journal of Writing and Writing Courses*, vol. 18, no. 1, 2014, http://www.textjournal.com.au/april14/gandolfo.htm

Gildersleeve, Jessica. *Christos Tsiolkas: The Utopian Vision.* Cambria P, 2017.

Giles, Fiona. "Milkbrain: Writing the Cognitive Body." *Australian Humanities Review*, vol. 43, 2007, http://australianhumanitiesreview.org/2007/12/01/milkbrain-writing-the-cognitive-body/.

Hayles, Katherine. "Greg Egan's Quarantine and Teranesia: Contributions to the Millennial Reassessment of Consciousness and the Cognitive Nonconscious." *Science Fiction Studies*, vol. 42, no. 1, 2015, pp. 56–77.

Heister, Hilmar. "Empathy and the Sympathetic Imagination in the Fiction of JM Coetzee." *Media Tropes*, vol. 4, no. 2, 2014, pp. 98–113.

Kimberley, Maree. "Neuroscience and Young Adult Fiction: A Recipe For Trouble." *M/C Journal*, vol. 14, no. 3, 2011, http://www.journal.media-culture.org.au/index.php/mcjournal/article/view/371

Mudiyanselage, Kumarasinghe Dissanayake. "Encouraging Empathy through Picture Books about Migration." *Picture Books and Beyond*, edited by Kerry Mallan. Primary English Teaching Association Australia, 201, pp. 75–91.

Mundell, Meg. "Crafting 'Literary Sense of Place': The Generative Work of Literary Place-Making." *JASAL*, vol. 18, no. 1, 2018, https://openjournals.library.sydney.edu.au/index.php/JASAL/article/viewFile/12375/11762

Newton, Pamela. "Beyond the Sensation Novel: Social Crime Fiction and Qualia of the Real World." *Literature and Sensation*, edited by Anthony Uhlmann, Helen Groth, Paul Sheehan, and Stephen McLaren. Cambridge Scholars Publishing, 2009, pp. 34–49.

Pettitt, Joanne. "On Blends and Abstractions: Children's Literature and the Mechanisms of Holocaust Representation." *International Research in Children's Literature*, vol. 7, no. 2, 2014, pp. 152–164.

Prendergast, Julia. "Grinding the Moor – Ideasthesia and Narrative." *New Writing*, vol. 15, no. 4, 2018, pp. 416–432.

Prendergast, Julia. "Narrative and the Unthought Known: The Immaterial Intelligence of Form." *TEXT*, vol. 23, no. 1, 2019, https://www.textjournal.com.au/april19/prendergast.htm.

Prendergast, Julia. "Ideasthetic Imagining—Patterns and Deviations in Affective Immersion." *New Writing: The International Journal for the Practice and Theory of Creative Writing*, 2020, https://www.tandfonline.com/doi/abs/10.1080/14790726.2019.1709508

Reeve, Victoria. "Emotion and Narratives of Heartland: Kim Scott's Benang and Peter Carey's Jack Maggs." *JASAL*, vol. 12, no. 3, 2013, https://openjournals.library.sydney.edu.au/index.php/JASAL/article/view/9830/9718

Robertson, Rachel. "'Driven by Tens': Obsession and Cognitive Difference in Toni Jordan's Romantic Comedy Addition." *Australasian Journal of Popular Culture*, vol. 3, no. 3, 2014, pp. 311–320.

Rubik, Margarete. "Provocative and Unforgettable: Peter Carey's Short Fiction." *European Journal of English Studies*, vol. 9, no. 2, 2005, pp. 169–184.

Spencer, Beth. *The Body as Fiction/Fiction as a Way of Thinking*. Unpublished PhD diss. University of Ballarat, 2006.

Spencer, Beth. "A Response to Fiona Giles, 'Milkbrain: Writing the Cognitive Body.'" *Australian Humanities Review*, vol. 43, 2007, http://australianhumanitiesreview.org/2007/12/01/a-response-to-fiona-giles-milkbrain-writing-the-cognitive-body/.

Stasny, Angélique. "Settler-Indigenous Relationships and the Emotional Regime of Empathy in Australian History School Textbooks in Times of Reconciliation." *Emotion, Affective Practices, and the Past in the Present*, edited by Laurajane Smith, Margaret Wetherell, and Gary Campbell. Routledge, 2018, pp. 246–264.

Stephens, John. "Writing *by* Children, Writing *for* Children: Schema Theory, Narrative Discourse and Ideology." *Crossing the Boundaries*, edited by Michèle Anstey and Geoff Bull. Pearson Education, 2002, pp. 237–248.

Stephens, John. "Affective Strategies, Emotion Schemas, and Empathic Endings: Selkie Girls and a Critical Odyssey." *Explorations into Children's Literature*, vol. 23, no. 1, 2015, pp. 17–33.

Stephens, John. "Picturebooks and Ideology." *The Routledge Companion to Picturebooks*, edited by Bettina Kümmerling-Meibauer. Routledge, 2017, pp. 137–145.

Takolander, Maria. "After Romanticism, Psychoanalysis and Postmodernism: New Paradigms for Theorising Creativity." *TEXT*, vol. 18, no. 2, 2014, http://www.textjournal.com.au/oct14/takolander.htm.

Takolander, Maria. "Dissanayake's 'Motherese' and Poetic Praxis: Theorising Emotion and Inarticulacy." *Axon*, vol. 4, no. 1, 2014, http://www.axonjournal.com.au/issue-6/dissanayake's-'motherese'-and-poetic-praxis.

Takolander, Maria. "A Dark/Inscrutable Workmanship: Shining a 'Scientific' Light on Emotion and Poiesis." *Axon Capsule*, vol. 1, 2015, http://www.axonjournal.com.au/issue-c1/darkinscrutable-workmanship.

Takolander, Maria. "From the 'Mad' Poet to the 'Embodied' Poet: Reconceptualising Creativity through Cognitive Science Paradigms." *TEXT*, vol. 19, no. 2, 2015, http://www.textjournal.com.au/oct15/takolander.htm.

Thomas, Diana Mary Eva. *Textiles in Text: Synaesthesia, Metaphor and Affect in Fiction*. Cambridge Scholars Publishing, 2017.

Vernay, Jean-François. *Neurocognitive Interpretations of Australian Literature: Criticism in the Age of Neuroawareness*. Routledge, 2021.

Vernay, Jean-François. "Forever in the Postcolonial Process of Growing Up: Change and Changelessness in Christopher Koch's Bildungsroman-Inspired Novels." *The Journal of the European Association of Studies on Australia*, vol. 10, no. 1, 2019, http://www.australianstudies.eu/?p=1344

Vernay, Jean-François. "Towards A New Direction in Contemporary Criticism: Cognitive Australian Literary Studies." *The Routledge Companion to Australian Literature*, edited by Jessica Gildersleeve. Routledge, 2020, pp. 116–122.

Research Theses

Harris, David Sydney. *Contemporary Australian Novels and Crises of Ecologies*. Unpublished PhD diss. Deakin University, 2017.

Heister, Hilmar. *The Sympathetic Imagination in the Novels of J.M.Coetzee: Empathy and Mirror Neurons in Literature*. Unpublished PhD diss. Humboldt University of Berlin, 2015.

Klein, Dorothee. *The Poetics and Politics of Relationality in Contemporary Australian Aboriginal Fiction*. Unpublished PhD diss. University of Stuttgart, 2019.

Mudiyanselage, Kumarasinghe Dissanayake. *The Role of Picture Books in Developing an Empathic Response Towards Cultural Difference*. Unpublished PhD diss. Queensland University of Technology, 2016.

Smith, Yvonne Joy. *Brightness Under Our Shoes: The Redress of the Poetic Imagination in the Poetry and Prose of David Malouf: 1960-1982*. PhD diss. University of Sydney, 2008.

Spencer, Beth. *The Body as Fiction/ Fiction as a Way of Thinking*. Unpublished PhD diss. University of Ballarat, 2006.

Stevens, Christopher David. *Crooked Paths to Insight: The Pragmatic of Loose and Tight Construing*. Unpublished PhD diss. University of Wollongong, 1999.

Thomas, Diana Mary Eva. *Textiles in Text: Synaesthesia, Metaphor and Affect in Fiction*. PhD diss. University of Wollongong, 2014.

Journalism

Fitzpatrick, Claire. "Neuroscience in Science Fiction: Brain Augmentation in an Increasingly Futuristic World." *Aurealis*, vol. 105, 2017, pp. 29–32.

Vernay, Jean-François. "Aspies Rule: Empowering Neurodivergence Fiction." Features Section, *The Adelaide Review*, 22 July 2019, p. 11.

Index

www.ingramcontent.com/pod-product-compliance
Ingram Content Group UK Ltd.
Pitfield, Milton Keynes, MK11 3LW, UK
UKHW020418010325
455677UK00029B/932